Isabel E Cohen

Readings and Recitations for Jewish Homes and Schools

Isabel E Cohen

Readings and Recitations for Jewish Homes and Schools

ISBN/EAN: 9783337032708

Printed in Europe, USA, Canada, Australia, Japan

Cover: Foto ©Thomas Meinert / pixelio.de

More available books at **www.hansebooks.com**

Readings and Recitations

FOR

JEWISH HOMES AND SCHOOLS

COMPILED BY

ISABEL E. COHEN

PHILADELPHIA
THE JEWISH PUBLICATION SOCIETY OF AMERICA
1895

PREFACE

The object in making the present collection is to provide matter suitable for reading and recitation in Sabbath-schools and Sunday-schools, at entertainments of Jewish societies, and in the home circle. Incidentally there has been an endeavor to illustrate some phases of Hebrew history and character, and to show the influence for good that the Bible of the Jews has had upon the history and literature of the English-speaking peoples.

The difficulties in making selections from the available material have not been few; nor does the compiler expect her judgment to meet with approval from every one.

It is believed that nothing altogether devoid of literary merit has been admitted, and it is hoped that the presence of familiar and even hackneyed poems and excerpts will be excused for their beauty or appropriateness.

I. E. C.

Philadelphia, November, 1893.

ACKNOWLEDGMENT

The Publication Committee acknowledges its indebtedness to the following publishers and authors, who have permitted the use of copyrighted matter:

MESSRS. D. APPLETON & CO., New York.—*Bryant's Song of the Stars*, and "*No Man knoweth of his Sepulchre.*"

MESSRS. HARPER & BROTHERS, New York.—*Humboldt's Descriptions of Nature in the Hebrew Writers* (from *Cosmos*); extracts from *Charles Reade's Bible Characters*.

MESSRS. HOUGHTON, MIFFLIN & CO., Boston (by arrangement with them).—*Aldrich's Judith* (extract), and *The Jew's Gift* (from *Mercedes and Later Lyrics*); *Browning's Saul* (extract); *George Anson Jackson's Legend of Iyob the Upright* (from *The Son of a Prophet*); *Emma Lazarus's Bar Kochba; The Crowing of the Red Cock; The Banner of the Jew*, and extracts from *The Dance to Death; Longfellow's Azrael, The Legend of Rabbi Ben Levi, Sandalphon*, and extracts from *Judas Maccabæus; Whittier's The Cities of the Plain, The Wife of Manoah to her Husband, Ezekiel*, and *The Two Rabbins*.

MESSRS. LONGMANS, GREEN & CO., New York.—*B. W. Richardson's A Legend of Paradise* (from *The Son of a Star*).

MESSRS. ROBERTS BROTHERS, Boston.—*Edwin Arnold's Azar and Abraham, Abraham's Bread*, and *Ozair the Jew* (from *Pearls of the Faith, or Islam's Rosary*).

Also to the following for the use of works published by them:

MESSRS. D. APPLETON & CO., New York.—*Grace Aguilar's The Pharisees* (from *Women of Israel*).

MESSRS. WILLIAM BLACKWOOD & SONS, London.—*David Kaufmann's The Future of Judaism* (from *George Eliot and Judaism*).

MESSRS. J. M. DENT & CO., London.—*Mrs. Henry Lucas's Translation of the Ode to Zion* (from *Songs of Zion*).

MR. JOHN HIGHLANDS, Philadelphia.—*Horatio Bonar's Mount Hor*.

MESSRS. MACMILLAN & CO., New York.—*Matthew Arnold's Israel and his Revelation* (from *Literature and Dogma*).

MESSRS. G. P. PUTNAM'S SONS, New York.—*Israel as Bride and as Beggar*, and *Forgiven* (from *Joseph Jacobs's Jews of Angevin England*).

MESSRS. GEORGE ROUTLEDGE & SONS, New York.—*E. H. Plumptre's The Water of Bethlehem Gate* (from *Three Cups of Cold Water*), and an extract from *The Queen of the South*.

CONTENTS

			PAGE
1	THE FUTURE OF JUDAISM (From *George Eliot and Judaism*)	DAVID KAUFMANN	13
2	THE HARP THE MONARCH MINSTREL SWEPT	LORD BYRON	18
3	PSALM IV	JOHN MILTON	19
4	PSALM XXIII	GEORGE HERBERT	20
5	PSALM XXVII	JAMES MONTGOMERY	21
6	PSALM XLII	JAMES MONTGOMERY	22
7	PSALM LXXX	BIBLE—REVISED VERSION	23
8	PSALM CXXI	JAMES MONTGOMERY	25
9	SONG OF REBECCA THE JEWESS (From *Ivanhoe*)	SIR WALTER SCOTT	26
10	DESCRIPTIONS OF NATURE IN THE HEBREW WRITERS (From *Cosmos*)	ALEXANDER VON HUMBOLDT	27
11	THOU ART, O GOD	THOMAS MOORE	31
12	THE SPACIOUS FIRMAMENT ON HIGH	JOSEPH ADDISON	32
13	SONG OF THE STARS	WILLIAM CULLEN BRYANT	33
14	VIEW OF PARADISE (From *Paradise Lost*)	JOHN MILTON	35
15	TUBAL CAIN	CHARLES MACKAY	38
16	AZAR AND ABRAHAM	EDWIN ARNOLD	40
17	ABRAHAM'S BREAD	EDWIN ARNOLD	41
18	ABRAHAM AND THE FIRE-WORSHIPPER	LEIGH HUNT	44

		PAGE
19	THE CITIES OF THE PLAIN JOHN GREENLEAF WHITTIER	48
20	BENJAMIN ACCOMPANIES HIS BRETHREN TO EGYPT BIBLE—LEESER'S TRANSLATION	50
21	JOSEPH AND HIS BRETHREN BIBLE—LEESER'S TRANSLATION	55
22	PASSAGE OF THE RED SEA . REGINALD HEBER	58
23	SONG OF MOSES . BIBLE—REVISED VERSION	59
24	MOUNT HOR . . . HORATIUS BONAR	62
25	BURIAL OF MOSES . . C. F. ALEXANDER	66
26	WEEP, CHILDREN OF ISRAEL . THOMAS MOORE	68
27	"NO MAN KNOWETH OF HIS SEPULCHRE" WILLIAM CULLEN BRYANT	69
28	DEBORAH'S SONG . BIBLE—REVISED VERSION	70
29	THE WIFE OF MANOAH TO HER HUSBAND JOHN GREENLEAF WHITTIER	73
30	DEATH OF SAMSON (From *Samson Agonistes*) . JOHN MILTON	77
31	RUTH . . . . . . THOMAS HOOD	79
32	THE CHILD SAMUEL . . J. D. BORTHWICK	80
33	SAUL (Extract) . . . ROBERT BROWNING	81
34	THE WATER OF BETHLEHEM GATE (From *Three Cups of Cold Water*) . E. H. PLUMPTRE	87
35	THE RAISING OF SAMUEL . . LORD BYRON	90
36	SONG OF SAUL BEFORE HIS LAST BATTLE LORD BYRON	92
37	DAVID'S LAMENT OVER SAUL AND JONATHAN BIBLE—REVISED VERSION	92
38	THE SONGS OF THE NIGHT THE HEBREW REVIEW	94
39	THE DEDICATION OF THE TEMPLE BIBLE—LEESER'S TRANSLATION	96
40	AZRAEL (Spanish Jew's Tale in *Tales of a Wayside Inn*) HENRY WADSWORTH LONGFELLOW	101
41	THE POOLS OF SOLOMON (From *Tancred*) . BENJAMIN DISRAELI	103
42	THE QUEEN OF THE SOUTH (Extract) . . . E. H. PLUMPTRE	106

CONTENTS

			PAGE
43	THE YOUTHFUL AND THE AGED SOLOMON	THE HEBREW REVIEW	110
44	ELIJAH'S INTERVIEW	CAMPBELL	113
45	ELIJAH	THE HEBREW REVIEW	115
46	OH! WEEP FOR THOSE	LORD BYRON	117
47	THE JEWISH CAPTIVE.	ELIZABETH OAKES SMITH	118
48	IDOLATRY.	BIBLE—LEESER'S TRANSLATION	121
49	THE FALSE GODS (From *Paradise Lost*).	JOHN MILTON	122
50	THE CAPTIVITY (From *Bible Characters*)	CHARLES READE	126
51	BY THE RIVERS OF BABYLON WE SAT DOWN AND WEPT	LORD BYRON	128
52	BUT WHO SHALL SEE	THOMAS MOORE	129
53	A PRAYER OF TOBIAS	MICHAEL DRAYTON	129
54	VISION OF BELSHAZZAR	LORD BYRON	132
55	BELSHAZZAR	B. W. PROCTOR	134
56	EZEKIEL	JOHN GREENLEAF WHITTIER	135
57	LEGEND OF IVOB THE UPRIGHT (From *The Son of a Prophet*)	GEORGE ANSON JACKSON	139
58	JUDITH AND HOLOFERNES (From *Judith*)	THOMAS BAILEY ALDRICH	142
59	THE PRAYER OF MARDOCHEUS	MICHAEL DRAYTON	147
60	NEHEMIAH (From *Bible Characters*)	CHARLES READE	148
61	NEHEMIAH, REFORMER (From *Bible Characters*)	CHARLES READE	153
62	MAHALA AND HER SEVEN SONS (From *Judas Maccabæus*)	HENRY WADSWORTH LONGFELLOW	156
63	JUDAS MACCABÆUS (From *Judas Maccabæus*)	HENRY WADSWORTH LONGFELLOW	164
64	THE BATTLE OF BETH-HORON (From *Judas Maccabæus*)	HENRY WADSWORTH LONGFELLOW	167

CONTENTS

			PAGE
65	THE PHARISEES (From *Women of Israel*)		
		GRACE AGUILAR	170
66	LINES FOR THE NINTH OF AB		
		SOLOMON SOLIS-COHEN	173
67	THE WILD GAZELLE . . .	LORD BYRON	174
68	OZAIR THE JEW . . .	EDWIN ARNOLD	175
69	BAR KOCHBA	EMMA LAZARUS	178
70	IN EXILE		
	(From *Synagogale Poesie des Mittelalters* by Leopold Zunz) . . .	RABBI JOSEPH	178
71	THE FIRST CRUSADE		
	(From *Synagogale Poesie des Mittelalters* by Leopold Zunz) .	KALONYMOS BEN JEHUDA	179
72	THE JEWS OF YORK		
	(From *Curiosities of Literature*).		
		ISAAC DISRAELI	181
73	TRIAL OF REBECCA (From *Ivanhoe*)		
		SIR WALTER SCOTT	187
74	THE JEW'S GIFT .	THOMAS BAILEY ALDRICH	199
75	PLEA FOR THE JEWS BEFORE THE COUNCIL AT NORDHAUSEN		
	(From *The Dance to Death*) .	EMMA LAZARUS	202
76	EXHORTATION TO THE JEWS OF NORDHAUSEN		
	(From *The Dance to Death*) .	EMMA LAZARUS	206
77	THE EXPULSION OF THE JEWS FROM SPAIN		
	(From *Coningsby*) .	BENJAMIN DISRAELI	209
78	OF THE PROPHECIES CONCERNING THE DISPERSION AND RESTORATION OF THE JEWS (From *Discourses on the Evidence of Revealed Religion*)	JOSEPH PRIESTLEY	214
79	CIVIL DISABILITIES OF THE JEWS		
	(Extract from Speech) . .	T. B. MACAULAY	219
80	CIVIL DISABILITIES OF THE JEWS		
	(Extract)	T. B. MACAULAY	224
81	THE CROWING OF THE RED COCK		
		EMMA LAZARUS	232
82	THE BANNER OF THE JEW	EMMA LAZARUS	233

CONTENTS

		PAGE
83	THE LEGEND OF RABBI BEN LEVI (Spanish Jew's Tale in *Tales of a Wayside Inn*) HENRY WADSWORTH LONGFELLOW	235
84	SANDALPHON HENRY WADSWORTH LONGFELLOW	237
85	THE RABBI'S VISION . . FRANCES BROWNE	239
86	THE TWO RABBINS JOHN GREENLEAF WHITTIER	243
87	A LEGEND OF PARADISE (From *The Son of a Star*) BENJAMIN WARD RICHARDSON	246
88	THE DYING HEBREW'S PRAYER (From *The Devil's Progress*) THOMAS KEBLE HERVEY	253
89	A JEWISH FAMILY . WILLIAM WORDSWORTH	258
90	THE WEEK (From *Bible Characters*) CHARLES READE	259
91	FRIDAY NIGHT . SOLOMON SOLIS-COHEN	260
92	THE SABBATH (From *The Genius of Judaism*) ISAAC DISRAELI	263
93	SABBATH IN THE JEWISH CAMP (From *Alroy*) BENJAMIN DISRAELI	265
94	ODE TO ZION . . . . JEHUDA HALEVI	267
95	SABBATH, MY LOVE . . . JEHUDA HALEVI	271
96	THE HARVEST FESTIVAL (From *Tancred*) . BENJAMIN DISRAELI	272
97	ISRAEL AND HIS REVELATION (From *Literature and Dogma*) . . . MATTHEW ARNOLD	276
98	ISRAEL AS BRIDE AND AS BEGGAR (From *Jews of Angevin England*, by Joseph Jacobs) . . . . ELCHANAN	277
99	"FORGIVEN" (From *Jews of Angevin England*, by Joseph Jacobs) . . . YOMTOB OF YORK	278
100	JEWISH NATIONALITY (From *Daniel Deronda*) . GEORGE ELIOT	280

> "And so I penned
> It down, until at last it came to be,
> For length and breadth, the bigness which you see."
>
> —JOHN BUNYAN.

THE FUTURE OF JUDAISM

(From *George Eliot and Judaism*)

Destroyed as the national independence of Judea was by Rome, from the bones of the vanquished there had already arisen—the Avenger; a branch severed from the parent trunk became a rod of correction for the oppressor; and a solitary Jewish idea sufficed, in its disfigurement, to shatter the Roman Mythology and all its faded splendor. And that idea arose to unimagined power, and rolled ever on and on like an avalanche, crushing the states over which it passed. But though it conquered the world, it remained without effect on those who were its originators. Banished from their home, they spread abroad over every land, outwardly disunited, inwardly at one. The Rigid in motion, the Eternal in transition, they advanced through time, deaf to all allurements, hardened against all oppression, and, as it were, insensible. They accepted their destiny as a dark necessity; they did not ask—why? They had a task; they *were forced* to live and to transmit downwards as an inheritance the inviolable legacy left them by the nations. Their path was marked by blood and tears; but faith in the final victory of truth glowed among them; and they believed— they knew—that with them alone did the truth abide. Thus, harassed by all, they have survived all; and when the dawn of a happier age began to break for them as for others, it illuminated a people numerically greater after eighteen hundred years of oppression and persecution than in the days of its highest power, and a race able to enrich every literature of the world from its treasures, even after men had inhumanly and treacherously sought to deprive its mental life of light and air. . . . . . .

It is more, however, by the question of the future of the Jews than by the enigma of their marvellous preservation that public reflection is demanded. Is the end and result of their glorious history to be their fusion and disappearance among the nations of the earth? Why then all this loving care? Why these grievous chains? Why these streams of blood and tears? Is this despised minority, from whose womb have sprung the religions which rule mankind, still to be called upon, at the grave of her daughters, to comfort and lift up a despairing world? Or will the semblance of unity which even now, if invisibly, binds together her dismembered limbs, grow paler and paler in the sunlight of progress? Will the hopes with which the thirsty have for centuries allayed their pangs keep ever running drier and drier, and finally shrink to the miserable remnant to which they are compared by shallow merriment? Are the Jews still a people, a sickly body, indeed, but one to whom youth and health may return, or a bleached and scattered heap of bones? Are these bones destined ever again to live and move? . . . .

No one will maintain that faith has soared to any very great elevation among the Jews, in recent decades; nevertheless, in comparison with earlier times, figures prove that apostasy has become rare among them. The reason usually alleged is, that their increasing liberty and ameliorated condition render that step superfluous; but fully to explain the fact, it must be noted that the Jews themselves have begun to recognize a *nationality* in Judaism—and a nationality which cannot be laid aside like a garment.

What will follow this awakening? Will that force inherent in the idea of nationality, which leads to the formation of States, and which, in recent times, has so wonderfully transformed the map of Europe, impel the Jews also to be in earnest with the hopes of thousands of years, and turn their patient longings into rapid actions? Will the march of history lead them, after all their wanderings and sufferings, to re-establish a definite centre and solemnly to complete their outward and visible unification? On this point the Jews are divided into two camps. For the one party the hope of rebuilding the ancient State is a childish and ridiculous enthusiast's dream, and the desire for a return to Sion an empty lie, for the obliteration of which from all forms of prayer moral duty calls, if truthfulness before the Almighty is to be respected; for the other party these longings are as the breath of Jewish national life, and their expression is a sacred command, and an inviolable law. In spite of all blustering and quarrelling, however, the fact cannot be denied that, for the *greater* portion of the Jews, Palestine is something more than a mere geographical notion; and that all the weaning of centuries, and all the enlightenment of modern times, have been unable to banish a longing for that land from their hearts, or to destroy the memory of it in their thoughts. . . .

The events of universal history are not to be estimated either by the short-sightedness of the Philistine or by the narrow-sightedness of the student. When the hour was ripe the Augustine monk became the father of the Reformation. The death of Islamism had been already proclaimed, when the Wahabees burst forth from their mountain fastnesses, and flamed through Arabia with a religious fervor unknown in modern times—a warning and a lesson to men not to class even Mohammedanism with the things of the past. Has not the Sick Man become proverbial? Have not political star-gazers foretold the very moment of his last death-rattle? A statesman like Midhat Pasha shows the world what sort of forces can be set in motion by a State tottering on the very verge of ruin. And Jewish history itself? The nine times Wise of the Babylonian Captivity smiled contemptuously at the fire of the prophets, and looked down with pity on the miserable creatures whose crazy infatuation it was to rebuild the temple. But from the midst of these very sufferers there arose minds to herald a new epoch for Judah, and to bring immortality to Judaism. And even when the race again lay broken on the ground, borne down with meek submissiveness beneath the Roman yoke, there blazed forth Bar Kochba, the Son of the Star, and hosts of devoted warriors sprang from the earth, compelling Rome to send her ablest commander to coerce them, a handful though they were. Nor did the inhuman lord of oppression set his iron heel upon the backs of the vanquished till streams of the blood of Judah's heroes had flowed down to the Mediterranean, and till treachery had crept in and broken their serried ranks. The defenders of Jerusalem and the heroes of Bethar did not surely bleed in vain! from the leonine uprising of Judea and from the safe and wondrous return of the exiles from the Babylonian Captivity, should not the lesson for all time be drawn, that the deep-rooted love and longing of the Jewish people for Palestine is something more than a wild and antiquated absurdity, something more than a barren dream of foolish enthusiasm? Feelings and sentiments which are worthy to be cherished and preserved in a nation's soul against all the influences of time are wont to concentrate themselves in great personalities, and to impart to them a power of attraction, before which moderation and half-heartedness fly like leaves before the storm. The history of

Israel presents a number of such figures. Ezra and Nehemiah succeed to the Prophets of the Captivity, John of Giskala stands beside Judas Maccabæus, Akiba ben Joseph defends the Star-Son of Bethar, and even through the darkness of the middle ages the fiery pillar of Jehudah ha-Levi gleams forth. Shall we some day be able to say— "and so on?"

DAVID KAUFMANN
Translation from the German by J. W. Ferrier

2

THE HARP THE MONARCH MINSTREL SWEPT

The harp the monarch minstrel swept,
   The King of men, the loved of Heaven,
Which music hallow'd while she wept
   O'er tones her heart of hearts had given,
   Redoubled be her tears, its cords are riven!
It soften'd men of iron mould,
   It gave them virtues not their own;
No ear so dull, no soul so cold,
   That felt not, fired not to the tone,
   Till David's lyre grew mightier than his throne!

It told the triumphs of our King,
   It wafted glory to our God;
It made our gladden'd valleys ring,
   The cedars bow, the mountains nod;

Its sound aspired to Heaven and there abode!
Since then, though heard on earth no more,
   Devotion and her daughter Love
Still bid the bursting spirit soar
   To sounds that seem as from above,
   In dreams that day's broad light cannot remove.

LORD BYRON

3

PSALM IV

Answer me when I call,
   God of my righteousness;
   In straits and in distress
Thou didst me disenthrall
   And set at large: now spare,
Now pity me, and hear my earnest prayer.
Great ones, how long will ye
   My glory have in scorn?
   How long be thus forborne
Still to love vanity?
   To love, to seek, to prize,
Things false and vain and nothing else but lies?
Yet know the Lord hath chose,
   Chose to himself apart,
   The good and meek of heart
(For whom to choose he knows);
   Jehovah from on high
Will hear my voice, what time to him I cry.
Be awed, and do not sin;

Speak to your hearts alone
Upon your beds, each one,
And be at peace within.
Offer the offerings just
Of righteousness, and in Jehovah trust.
Many there be that say
Who yet will show us good?
Talking like this world's brood;
But, Lord, thus let me pray;
On us lift up the light,
Lift up the favor, of thy count'nance bright.
Into my heart more joy
And gladness thou hast put
Than when a year of glut
Their stores doth over-cloy,
And from their plenteous grounds
With vast increase their corn and wine abounds.
In peace at once will I
Both lay me down and sleep;
For thou alone dost keep
Me safe where'er I lie:
As in a rocky cell
Thou, Lord! alone, in safety mak'st me dwell.

JOHN MILTON

4

THE TWENTY-THIRD PSALME

The God of love my shepherd is,
And he that doth me feed:
While he is mine, and I am his,
What can I want or need?

He leads me to the tender grasse,
  Where I both feed and rest ;
Then to the streams that gently pass :
  In both I have the best.

Or if I stray, he doth convert,
  And bring my minde in frame :
And all this not for my desert
  But for his holy name.

Yea, in death's shadie black abode
  Well may I walk, not fear :
For thou art with me, and thy rod
  To guide, thy staffe to bear.

Nay, thou dost make me sit and dine,
  Ev'n in my enemies' sight :
My head with oyl, my cup with wine
  Runnes over day and night.

Surely thy sweet and wondrous love
  Shall measure all my dayes ;
And as it never shall remove
  So neither shall my praise.

GEORGE HERBERT

5

PSALM XXVII

God is my strong salvation,
  What foe have I to fear ?
In darkness and temptation,
  My light, my help is near :

Though hosts encamp around me,
    Firm to the fight I stand;
What terror can confound me,
    With God at my right hand?

Place on the Lord reliance,
    My soul, with courage wait;
His truth be thine affiance,
    When faint and desolate:

His might thine heart shall strengthen,
    His love thy joy increase;
Mercy thy days shall lengthen;
    The Lord will give thee peace.

JAMES MONTGOMERY

6

PSALM XLII

Hearken, Lord, to my complaints,
For my soul within me faints;
Thee, far off, I call to mind,
In the land I left behind,
Where the streams of Jordan flow,
Where the heights of Hermon glow.

Tempest-tost, my failing bark
Founders on the ocean dark;
Deep to deep around me calls,
With the rush of water-falls;
While I plunge to lower caves,
Overwhelm'd by all thy waves.

Once the morning's earliest light
Brought thy mercy to my sight,
And my wakeful song was heard
Later than the evening bird;
Hast thou all my prayers forgot?
Dost thou scorn, or hear them not?

Why, my soul, art thou perplex'd?
Why with faithless trouble vex'd?
Hope in God, whose saving name
Thou shalt joyfully proclaim,
When his countenance shall shine
Through the clouds that darken thine.

JAMES MONTGOMERY

7

PSALM LXXX

Give ear, O Shepherd of Israel,
Thou that leadest Joseph like a flock;
Thou that sittest upon the cherubim, shine forth.
Before Ephraim and Benjamin and Manasseh, stir up thy might,
And come to save us.
Turn us again, O God;
And cause thy face to shine, and we shall be saved.

O Lord God of hosts,
How long wilt thou be angry against the prayer of thy people?
Thou hast fed them with the bread of tears,
And given them tears to drink in large measure.

Thou makest us a strife unto our neighbors :
And our enemies laugh among themselves.
Turn us again, O God of hosts ;
And cause thy face to shine, and we shall be saved.
Thou broughtest a vine out of Egypt :
Thou didst drive out the nations, and plantedst it.
Thou preparedst room before it,
And it took deep root, and filled the land.
The mountains were covered with the shadow of it,
And the boughs thereof were like cedars of God.
She sent out her branches unto the sea,
And her shoots unto the River.
Why hast thou broken down her fences,
So that all they which pass by the way do pluck her?
The boar out of the wood doth ravage it,
And the wild beasts of the field feed on it.
Turn again, we beseech thee, O God of hosts :
Look down from heaven, and behold, and visit this vine,
And the stock which thy right hand hath planted,
And the branch that thou madest strong for thyself.
It is burned with fire, it is cut down :
They perish at the rebuke of thy countenance.
Let thy hand be upon the man of thy right hand,
Upon the son of man whom thou madest strong for thyself.
So shall we not go back from thee :
Quicken thou us, and we will call upon thy name.
Turn us again, O Lord God of hosts :
Cause thy face to shine, and we shall be saved.

BIBLE—REVISED VERSION

8

PSALM CXXI

Encompass'd with ten thousand ills,
   Press'd by pursuing foes,
I lift mine eyes unto the hills,
   From whence salvation flows.

My help is from the Lord, who made
   And governs earth and sky;
I look to his almighty aid,
   And ever-watching eye.

He who my soul in safety keeps
   Shall drive destruction hence;
The Lord thy keeper never sleeps;
   The Lord is thy defence.

The sun, with his afflictive light,
   Shall harm thee not by day;
Nor thee the moon molest by night
   Along thy tranquil way.

Thee shall the Lord preserve from sin,
   And comfort in distress;
Thy going out and coming in,
   The Lord thy God shall bless.

JAMES MONTGOMERY

9

SONG OF REBECCA THE JEWESS

(From *Ivanhoe*)

When Israel, of the Lord beloved,
    Out from the land of bondage came,
Her fathers' God before her moved,
    An awful guide in smoke and flame.
By day, along the astonish'd lands
    The cloudy pillar glided slow;
By night, Arabia's crimson'd sands
    Return'd the fiery column's glow.

There rose the choral hymn of praise,
    And trump and timbrel answer'd keen,
And Zion's daughters pour'd their lays,
    With priest's and warrior's voice between.
No portents now our foes amaze,
    Forsaken Israel wanders lone:
Our fathers would not know *Thy* ways,
    And *Thou* hast left them to their own.

But, present still, though now unseen;
    When brightly shines the prosperous day,
Be thoughts of *Thee* a cloudy screen
    To temper the deceitful ray.
And oh, when stoops on Judah's path
    In shade and storm the frequent night,
Be *Thou*, long-suffering, slow to wrath,
    A burning, and a shining light.

Our harps we left by Babel's streams,
  The tyrant's jest, the Gentile's scorn :
No censer round our altar beams,
  And mute are timbrel, trump, and horn.
But *Thou* hast said, The blood of goat,
  The flesh of rams, I will not prize ;
A contrite heart, an humble thought,
  Are mine accepted sacrifice.

SIR WALTER SCOTT

10

DESCRIPTION OF NATURE IN THE HEBREW WRITERS

(From *Cosmos*)

It is a characteristic of the poetry of the Hebrews, that, as a reflex of monotheism, it always embraces the universe in its unity, comprising both terrestrial life and the luminous realms of space. It dwells but rarely on the individuality of phenomena, preferring the contemplation of great masses. The Hebrew poet does not depict nature as a self-dependent object, glorious in its individual beauty, but always as in relation and subjection to a higher spiritual power. Nature is to him a work of creation and order, the living expression of the omnipresence of the Divinity in the visible world. Hence the lyrical poetry of the Hebrews, from the very nature of its subject, is grand and solemn, and when it treats of the earthly condition of mankind, is full of sad and pensive longing. It is worthy of remark, that Hebrew poetry, notwithstanding its grandeur, and the lofty tone of exaltation to which it is often elevated by the charm of music, scarcely ever loses the restraint of measure, as does the poetry of India. Devoted to the pure contemplation of the Divinity, it remains clear and single in the midst of the most figurative forms of expression, delighting in comparisons which recur with almost rhythmical regularity.

As descriptions of nature, the writings of the Old Testament are a faithful reflection of the character of the country in which they were composed, of the alternations of barrenness and fruitfulness, and of the Alpine forests by which the land of Palestine was characterized. They describe in their regular succession the relations of the climate, the manners of this people of herdsmen, and their hereditary aversion to agricultural pursuits. The epic or historical narratives are marked by a graceful simplicity, almost more unadorned than those of Herodotus, and most true to nature; a point on which the unanimous testimony of modern travellers may be received as conclusive, owing to the inconsiderable changes effected in the course of ages in the manners and habits of a nomadic people. Their lyrical poetry is more adorned, and develops a rich and animated conception of the life of nature.

It might almost be said that one single psalm (the 104th) represents the image of the whole cosmos:

"Who coverest thyself with light as with a garment; who stretchest out the heavens like a curtain:

Who layeth the beams of his chambers in the waters: who maketh the clouds his chariot; who walketh upon the wings of the wind:

Who laid the foundations of the earth, that it should not be removed forever.

He sendeth the springs into the valleys, which run among the hills.

They give drink to every beast of the field: the wild asses quench their thirst.

By them shall the fowls of the heaven have their habitation, which sing among the branches.

He causeth the grass to grow for the cattle, and herb for the service of man: that he may bring forth food out of the earth;

And wine that maketh glad the heart of man, and oil to make his face to shine, and bread which strengtheneth man's heart.

The trees of the Lord are full of sap; the cedars of Lebanon which he hath planted;

Where the birds make their nests: as for the stork, the fir-trees are her house."

"The great and wide sea" is then described, "wherein are things creeping innumerable, both small and great beasts. There go the ships: there is that leviathan, whom thou hast made to play therein."

The description of the heavenly bodies renders this picture of nature complete:

"He appointed the moon for seasons: the sun knoweth his going down.

Thou makest darkness, and it is night; wherein all the beasts of the forest do creep forth.

The young lions roar after their prey, and seek their meat from God

The sun ariseth, they gather themselves together, and lay them down in their dens.

Man goeth forth unto his work and to his labor until the evening."

We are astonished to find, in a lyrical poem of such a limited compass, the whole universe—the heavens and the earth—sketched with a few bold touches. The calm and toilsome labor of man, from the rising of the sun to the setting of the same, when his daily work is done, is here contrasted with the moving life of the elements of nature. This contrast and generalization in the conception of the mutual action of natural phenomena, and this retrospection of an omnipresent invisible power, which can renew the earth or crumble it to dust, constitute a solemn and exalted rather than a glowing and gentle form of poetic creation. . . . .

The Book of Job is generally regarded as the most perfect specimen of the poetry of the Hebrews. It is alike picturesque in the delineation of individual phenomena, and artistically skilful in the didactic arrangement of the whole work. In all the modern languages into which the Book of Job has been translated, its images, drawn from the natural scenery of the East, leave a deep impression on the mind.

"The Lord walketh on the heights of the waters, on the ridges of the waves towering high beneath the force of the wind."

"The morning red has colored the margins of the earth, and variously formed the covering of clouds, as the hand of man moulds the yielding clay."

The habits of animals are described, as, for instance, those of the wild ass, the horse, the buffalo, the rhinoceros, and the crocodile, the eagle, and the ostrich. We see "the pure ether spread, during the scorching heat of the south wind, as a melted mirror over the parched desert."

ALEXANDER VON HUMBOLDT
Translation from the German by E. C. Otté

II

THOU ART, O GOD

The day is thine; the night also is thine; thou hast prepared the light and the sun. Thou hast set all the borders of the earth; thou hast made summer and winter.—PSALM lxxiv. 16, 17.

> Thou art, O God, the life and light
>   Of all this wondrous world we see;
> Its glow by day, its smile by night,
>   Are but reflections caught from thee.
> Where'er we turn, thy glories shine,
>   And all things fair and bright are thine.
>
> When day, with farewell beam, delays
>   Among the opening clouds of even,
> And we can almost think we gaze
>   Through golden vistas into heaven—
> Those hues, that make the sun's decline
>   So soft, so radiant, Lord! are thine.

When night, with wings of starry gloom,
    O'ershadows all the earth and skies,
Like some dark, beauteous bird, whose plume
    Is sparkling with unnumbered eyes—
That sacred gloom, those fires divine,
    So grand, so countless, Lord! are thine.

When youthful spring around us breathes,
    Thy spirit warms her fragrant sigh;
And every flower the summer wreathes
    Is born beneath that kindling eye.
Where'er we turn thy glories shine,
    And all things fair and bright are thine.

                  THOMAS MOORE

12

THE SPACIOUS FIRMAMENT ON HIGH

The spacious firmament on high,
With all the blue ethereal sky,
And spangled Heavens, a shining frame,
Their great Original proclaim.
Th' unwearied sun from day to day
Does his Creator's power display,
And publishes to every land
The work of an almighty hand.

Soon as the evening shades prevail,
The moon takes up the wondrous tale;
And nightly, to the list'ning earth,
Repeats the story of her birth:

Whilst all the stars that round her burn,
And all the planets, in their turn,
Confirm the tidings as they roll,
And spread the truth from pole to pole.

What though in solemn silence, all
Move round the dark terrestrial ball?
What though, nor real voice nor sound
Amid their radiant orbs be found?
In reason's ear they all rejoice,
And utter forth a glorious voice,
Forever singing as they shine,
"The hand that made us is divine."

JOSEPH ADDISON

13

SONG OF THE STARS

When the radiant morn of creation broke,
And the world in the smile of God awoke,
And the empty realms of darkness and death
Were moved through their depths by his mighty
    breath,
And orbs of beauty and spheres of flame
From the void abyss by myriads came—
In the joy of youth as they darted away,
Through the widening wastes of space to play,
Their silver voices in chorus rang,
And this was the song the bright ones sang:

"Away, away, through the wide, wide sky,
The fair blue fields that before us lie—
Each sun with the worlds that round him roll,
Each planet, poised on her turning pole;
With her isles of green, and her clouds of white,
And her waters that lie like fluid light.

"For the source of glory uncovers his face,
And the brightness o'erflows unbounded space,
And we drink as we go to the luminous tides
In our ruddy air and our blooming sides:
Lo, yonder the living splendors play;
Away, on our joyous path, away!

"Look, look, through our glittering ranks afar,
In the infinite azure, star after star,
How they brighten and bloom as they swiftly pass!
How the verdure runs o'er each rolling mass!
And the path of the gentle winds is seen,
Where the small waves dance, and the young woods
    lean.

"And see, where the brighter day-beams pour,
How the rainbows hang in the sunny shower;
And the morn and eve, with their pomp of hues,
Shift o'er the bright planets and shed their dews;
And 'twixt them both, o'er the teeming ground,
With her shadowy cone the night goes round!

"Away, away! in our blossoming bowers,
In the soft airs wrapping these spheres of ours,
In the seas and fountains that shine with the morn,
See, Love is brooding, and Life is born,

And breathing myriads are breaking from night,
To rejoice like us, in motion and light.

"Glide on in your beauty, ye youthful spheres,
To weave the dance that measures the years;
Glide on, in the glory and gladness sent,
To the furthest wall of the firmament—
The boundless visible smile of Him
To the veil of whose brow your lamps are dim."

WILLIAM CULLEN BRYANT

14

VIEW OF PARADISE

(From *Paradise Lost*)

. . . . In this pleasant soil
His far more pleasant garden God ordained.
Out of the fertile ground he caused to grow
All trees of noblest kind for sight, smell, taste;
And all amid them stood the Tree of Life,
High eminent, blooming ambrosial fruit
Of vegetable gold; and next to life,
Our death, the Tree of Knowledge, grew fast by—
Knowledge of good, bought dear by knowing ill.
Southward through Eden went a river large,
Nor changed his course, but through the shaggy hill
Passed underneath ingulfed; for God had thrown
That mountain as his garden-mould, high raised
Upon the rapid current, which, through veins
Of porous earth with kindly thirst up-drawn,

Rose a fresh fountain, and with many a rill
Watered the garden; thence united fell
Down the steep glade, and met the nether flood,
Which from his darksome passage now appears,
And now, divided into four main streams,
Runs diverse, wandering many a famous realm
And country, whereof here needs no account,
But rather to tell how, if Art could tell
How, from that sapphire fount the crispèd brooks,
Rolling on orient pearl and sands of gold,
With mazy error under pendent shades
Ran nectar, visiting each plant, and fed
Flowers worthy of Paradise, which not nice Art
In beds and curious knots, but Nature boon
Poured forth profuse on hill, and dale, and plain,
Both where the morning sun first warmly smote
The open field, and where the unpierced shade
Imbrowned the noontide bowers. Thus was this place,
A happy rural seat of various view:
Groves whose rich trees wept odorous gums and balm;
Others whose fruit, burnished with golden rind,
Hung amiable—Hesperian fables true,
If true, here only—and of delicious taste.
Betwixt them lawns, or level downs, and flocks
Grazing the tender herb, were interposed,
Or palmy hillock, or the flowery lap
Of some irriguous valley, spread her store,
Flowers of all hue, and without thorn the rose.
Another side, umbrageous grots and caves
Of cool recess, o'er which the mantling vine

Lays forth her purple grape, and gently creeps
Luxuriant; meanwhile murmuring waters fall
Down the slope hills, dispersed, or in a lake,
That to the fringèd bank with myrtle crowned
Her crystal mirror holds, unite their streams.
The birds their choir apply; airs, vernal airs,
Breathing the smell of field and grove, attune
The trembling leaves, while universal Pan,
Knit with the Graces and the Hours in dance,
Led on the eternal Spring. . . . . . .
Two of far nobler shape, erect and tall,
God-like erect, with native honor clad
In naked majesty, seemed lords of all,
And worthy seemed; for in their looks divine
The image of their glorious Maker shone,
Truth, wisdom, sanctitude severe and pure—
Severe, but in true filial freedom placed,
Whence true authority in men: though both
Not equal, as their sex not equal seemed ;
For contemplation he and valor formed,
For softness she and sweet attractive grace,
He for God only, she for God in him.
    . . . .
. . . . About them frisking played
All beasts of the earth, since wild, and of all chase
In wood or wilderness, forest or den.
Sporting the lion ramped, and in his paw
Dandled the kid; bears, tigers, ounces, pards,
Gambolled before them; the unwieldy elephant,
To make them mirth, used all his might, and
    wreathed
His lithe proboscis; close the serpent sly.

Insinuating, wove with Gordian twine
His braided train, and of his fatal guile
Gave proof unheeded. Others on the grass
Couched, and, now filled with pasture, gazing sat,
Or bedward ruminating.
JOHN MILTON

15

TUBAL CAIN

Old Tubal Cain was a man of might,
  In the days when earth was young;
By the fierce red light of his furnace bright,
  The strokes of his hammer rung;
And he lifted high his brawny hand
  On the iron glowing clear,
Till the sparks rushed out in scarlet showers,
  As he fashioned the sword and spear.
And he sang—" Hurrah for my handiwork!
  Hurrah for the spear and the sword!
Hurrah for the hand that shall wield them well,
  For he shall be king and lord!"

To Tubal Cain came many a one,
  As he wrought by his roaring fire,
And each one prayed for a strong steel blade,
  As the crown of his desire.
And he made them weapons sharp and strong,
  Till they shouted loud for glee,
And gave him gifts of pearl and gold,
  And spoils of the forest free.

And they sang—" Hurrah for Tubal Cain
  Who hath given us strength anew!
Hurrah for the smith, hurrah for the fire,
  And hurrah for the metal true!"

But a sudden change came o'er his heart
  Ere the setting of the sun;
And Tubal Cain was filled with pain
  For the evil he had done:
He saw that men, with rage and hate,
  Made war upon their kind,
That the land was red with the blood they shed,
  In their lust for carnage blind.
And he said—"Alas! that ever I made,
  Or that skill of mine should plan,
The spear and the sword, for men whose joy
  Is to slay their fellow-man."

And for many a day old Tubal Cain
  Sat brooding o'er his woe;
And his hand forbore to smite the ore,
  And his furnace smouldered low.
But he rose at last with a cheerful face,
  And a bright courageous eye,
And bared his strong right arm for work,
  While the quick flames mounted high.
And he sang—"Hurrah for my handiwork!"
  And the red sparks lit the air;
"Not alone for the blade was the bright steel made,"
  And he fashioned the first ploughshare.

And men, taught wisdom from the past,
  In friendship joined their hands,

Hung the sword in the hall, the spear on the wall,
  And ploughed the willing lands ;
And sang—" Hurrah for Tubal Cain !
  Our stanch good friend is he ;
And for the ploughshare and the plough,
  To him our praise shall be.
But while oppression lifts its head,
  Or a tyrant would be lord,
Though we may thank him for the plough,
  We'll not forget the sword."

CHARLES MACKAY

16

AZAR AND ABRAHAM

Azar, of Abraham the father, spake
Unto his son, "Come! and thine offerings make
Before the gods whose images divine
In Nimrûd's carved and painted temple shine.
Pay worship to the sun's great orb of gold ;
Adore the queen-moon's silver state ; behold
Otâred, Moshtari, Sohayl, in their might,
Those stars of glory, those high lords of light.
These have we wrought, as fitteth gods alone,
In bronze and ivory and chiselled stone.
Obey, as did thy sires, these powers of Heaven
Which rule the world, throned in the circles seven."

But Abraham said, " Did they not see the sun
Sink and grow darkened, when the days were done ;

Did not the moon for them, too, wax and wane,
That they should pay her worship, false and vain?
Lo! all these stars have laws to rise and set—
Otâred, Moshtari, Sohayl—wilt thou yet
Bid me praise gods who humbly come and go,
Lights that a Greater Light hath kindled? No!
I dare not bow the knee to one of these;
My Lord is He who (past the sky man sees)
Waxeth and waneth not, Unchanged of all,
Him only 'God,' Him only 'Great,' I call."

EDWIN ARNOLD

17

ABRAHAM'S BREAD

. . . . There had fall'n drought
Upon the land, and all the mouths he fed
Hungered for meal; therefore Al-Khalil sent
Messengers unto Egypt—to a Lord
Wealthy and favorable, having store
Of grain and cattle by the banks of Nile.
"Give unto Abraham," the message said,
"A little part for gold, yet more for love—
(As he had given, if the strait were thine)
Meal of the millet, lentil, wheat, and bean,
That he and his may live; for drought hath come
Upon our fields and pastures, and we pine."
Spake the Egyptian lord, "Lo! now ye ask
O'ermuch of me for friendliness, and more
Than gold can buy, since dearth hath also come

Over our fields, and nothing is to spare.
Yet had it been to succor Abraham,
And them that dwell beneath his tent, the half
Of all we hold had filled your empty sacks.
But he will feed people we wot not of,
Poor folk, and hungry wanderers of the waste;
The which are naught to us, who have of such,
If there were surplusage. Therefore return;
Find food elsewhere."
. . . . Then said the messengers
One to another, " If we shall return
With empty sacks, our master's name, so great
For worship in the world, will suffer shame,
And men will say he asked and was denied."
Therefore they filled their sacks with white sea-sand
Gathered by Gaza's wave, and sorrowfully
Journeyed to Kedar, where lay Abraham,
To whom full privately they told this thing,
Saying, "We filled the sacks with snow-white sand,
Lest thy great name be lessened 'mongst the folk,
Seeing us empty-handed; for the man
Denied thee corn; since thou wouldst give, quoth he,
To poor folk and to wanderers of the waste,
And there are hungry mouths enough by Nile."
Then was the heart of Abraham sore, because
The people of his tribe drew round to share
The good food brought, and all the desert trooped
With large-eyed mothers and their pining babes,
Certain of succor if the sheikh could help.

So did the spirit of Al-Khalil sink
That into swoon he fell and lay as one
Who hath not life. But Sarai, his wife —
That knew not — bade her maidens bring a sack,
Open its mouth, and knead some meal for cakes.
And when the sack was opened, there showed flour,
Fine, three times bolted, whiter than sea-sand;
Which in the trough they kneaded, rolling cakes,
And baking them over the crackling thorns;
So that the savor spread throughout the camp
Of new bread smoking, and the people drew
Closer and thicker, as ye see the herds
Throng — horn, and wool, and hoof — at watering-time,
When after fiery leagues, the wells are reached.
But Abraham, awaking, smelled the bread:
"Whence," spake he unto Sarai, "hast thou meal,
Wife of my bosom? for the smell of bread
Ariseth, and lo! I see the cakes are baked."
" By God! Who is the only One," she said,
"Whence should it come save from thy friend who sent,
The lord of Egypt?" "Nay!" quoth Abraham,
And fell upon his face, low-worshipping,
"But this hath come from the dear mighty hands
Of Allah — of the Lord of Egypt's lords —
My 'Friend,' and King, and Helper: now my folk
Shall live and die not. Glory be to God!"

EDWIN ARNOLD

18

ABRAHAM AND THE FIRE-WOR-SHIPPER

A DRAMATIC PARABLE

SCENE.—The inside of a tent in which the patriarch ABRAHAM and a PERSIAN TRAVELLER, a Fire-Worshipper, are sitting awhile after supper.

Fire-Worshipper [*aside*].   What have I said, or
　　done, that by degrees
Mine host hath changed his gracious countenance,
Until he stareth on me, as in wrath!
Have I, 'twixt wake and sleep, lost his wise lore?
Or sit I thus too long, and he himself
Would fain be sleeping?   I will speak to that.
(*Aloud*) Impute it, O my great and gracious lord,
Unto my feeble flesh, and not my folly,
If mine old eyelids droop against their will,
And I become as one that hath no sense
Ev'n to the milk and honey of thy words.—
With my lord's leave, and his good servant's help,
My limbs would creep to bed.
　　Abraham [*angrily quitting his seat*].   In this
　　　　tent, never.
Thou art a thankless and an impious man.
　　Fire-W. [*rising in astonishment*].   A thankless
　　　　and an impious man! Oh, sir,
My thanks have all but worshipp'd thee.
　　Abraham.　　　　　　　　　　And whom
Forgotten? like the fawning dog I feed.
From the foot-washing to the meal, and now

To this thy cramm'd and dog-like wish for bed,
I've noted thee; and never hast thou breath'd
One syllable of prayer, or praise, or thanks,
To the great God who made and feedeth all.

 Fire-W. Oh, sir, the God I worship is the Fire,
The god of gods; and seeing him not here,
In any symbol, or on any shrine,
I waited till he bless'd mine eyes at morn,
Sitting in heaven.

 Abraham. Oh, foul idolater!
And dare'st thou still to breathe in Abraham's tent?
Forth with thee, wretch: for he that made thy god,
And all thy tribe, and all the hosts of heaven,
The invisible and only dreadful God,
Will speak to thee this night, out in the storm,
And try thee in thy foolish god, the fire,
Which with his fingers he makes lightnings of.
Hark to the rising of his robes, the winds,
And get thee forth, and wait him.

      [*A violent storm is heard rising.*]

 Fire-W.   What! unhous'd!
And on a night like this! me, poor old man,
A hundred years of age!

 Abraham [*urging him away*]. Not reverencing
The God of ages, thou revoltest reverence.

 Fire-W. Thou had'st a father:—think of his gray
  hairs,
Houseless, and cuff'd by such a storm as this.

 Abraham. God is thy father and thou own'st not
  him.

 Fire-W. I have a wife, as aged as myself,
And if she learn my death, she'll not survive it,

No, not a day ; she is so used to me :
So propp'd up by her other feeble self.
I pray thee, strike not both down.
 Abraham [*still urging him*]. God made
Husband and wife, and must be own'd of them,
Else he must needs disown them.
 Fire-W.   We have children,
One of them, sir, a daughter, who, next week,
Will all day long be going in and out,
Upon the watch for me ; she too, a wife,
And will be soon a mother. Spare, O spare her !
She's a good creature, and not strong.
 Abraham.   Mine ears
Are deaf to all things but thy blasphemy,
And to the coming of the Lord and God,
Who will this night condemn thee.
[*Abraham pushes him out; and remains alone speaking.*]
          For if ever
God came at night-time forth upon the world,
'Tis now this instant. Hark to the huge winds,
The cataracts of hail, and rocky thunder,
Splitting like quarries of the stony clouds,
Beneath the touching of the foot of God.
That was God's speaking in the heavens,—that last
And inward utterance coming by itself.
What is it shaketh thus thy servant, Lord,
Making him fear, that in some loud rebuke
To this idolater, whom thou abhorrest,
Terror will slay himself ? Lo, the earth quakes
Beneath my feet, and God is surely here.
   [*A dead silence ; then a still small voice.*]

The Voice. Abraham!

Abraham. Where art thou, Lord? and who is it
that speaks
So sweetly in mine ear, to bid me turn
And dare to face thy presence?

The Voice. Who but He
Whose mightiest utterance thou hast yet to learn?
I was not in the whirlwind, Abraham;
I was not in the thunder, or the earthquake;
But I am in the still small voice.
Where is the stranger whom thou tookest in?

Abraham. Lord, he denied thee, and I drove him
forth.

The Voice. Then didst thou do what God himself forbore.
Have I, although he did deny me, borne
With his injuriousness these hundred years,
And could'st thou not endure him one sole night,
And such a night as this?

Abraham. Lord! I have sinn'd
And will go forth, and if he be not dead,
Will call him back, and tell him of thy mercies
Both to himself, and me.

The Voice. Behold, and learn!

[*The Voice retires while it is speaking; and a fold
of the tent is turned back disclosing the Fire-
Worshipper, who is calmly sleeping, with his
head on the back of a house-lamb.*]

Abraham. O loving God! the lamb itself's his
pillow,
And on his forehead is a balmy dew,
And in his sleep he smileth. I, meantime,

Poor and proud fool, with my presumptuous hands,
Not God's, was dealing judgments on his head,
Which God himself had cradled!—Oh, methinks
There's more in this than prophet yet hath known,
And Faith, some day, will all in Love be shown.

LEIGH HUNT

19

THE CITIES OF THE PLAIN

"Get ye up from the wrath of God's terrible day!
Ungirded, unsandalled, arise and away!
'Tis the vintage of blood, 'tis the fulness of time,
And vengeance shall gather the harvest of crime!"

The warning was spoken—the righteous had gone,
And the proud ones of Sodom were feasting alone;
All gay was the banquet—the revel was long,
With the pouring of wine and the breathing of song.

'Twas an evening of beauty; the air was perfume,
The earth was all greenness, the trees were all
    bloom;
And softly the delicate viol was heard,
Like the murmur of love or the notes of a bird.

And beautiful maidens moved down in the dance,
With the magic of motion and sunshine of glance;
And white arms wreathed lightly, and tresses fell
    free,
As the plumage of birds in some tropical tree.

Where the shrines of foul idols were lighted on high,
And wantonness tempted the lust of the eye;
'Midst rites of obsceneness, strange, loathsome, abhorred,
The blasphemer scoffed at the name of the Lord.

Hark! the growl of the thunder,—the quaking of earth!
Woe, woe to the worship, and woe to the mirth!
The black sky has opened; there's flame in the air;
The red arm of vengeance is lifted and bare!

Then the shriek of the dying rose wild where the song
And the low tone of love had been whispered along;
For the fierce flames went lightly o'er palace and bower,
Like the red tongues of demons, to blast and devour.

Down, down on the fallen the red ruin rained,
And the reveller sank with his wine-cup undrained;
The foot of the dancer, the music's loved thrill,
And the shout and the laughter grew suddenly still.

The last throb of anguish was fearfully given;
The last eye glared forth in its madness on Heaven!
The last groan of horror rose wildly and vain,
And death brooded over the pride of the Plain.

JOHN GREENLEAF WHITTIER

20

BENJAMIN ACCOMPANIES HIS BRETHREN TO EGYPT

Genesis xliii. 1-31; xliv. 1-17.

And the famine was sore in the land.

And it came to pass, when they had completely eaten up the provisions which they had brought out of Egypt, that their father said unto them, Go again, buy us a little food.

And Judah said unto him, thus, The man did solemnly protest unto us, saying, Ye shall not see my face except your brother be with you.

If thou wilt send our brother with us, we will go down and buy thee food;

But if thou sendest him not, we will not go down; for the man said unto us, Ye shall not see my face except your brother be with you.

And Israel said, Wherefore have ye dealt so ill with me, as to tell the man that ye have yet another brother?

And they said, The man inquired particularly concerning us, and our kindred, saying, Is your father yet alive? have ye another brother? and we told him according to the tenor of these words: could we possibly know that he would say, Bring down your brother?

And Judah said unto Israel his father, Send the lad with me, and we will arise and go; that we may live, and not die, both we, and thou, as also our little ones.

I will be surety for him; from my hand shalt thou require him: if I bring him not unto thee, and set him before thee, then shall I have sinned against thee all the days.

For, if we had not lingered, surely we had now returned the second time.

And their father Israel said unto them, If it must be so now, do this : take of the best products of the land in your vessels, and carry down to the man a present, a little balm, and a little honey, spices, and lotus, pistachio-nuts, and almonds.

And twofold money take in your hand ; and the money that was put back in the mouth of your sacks, you must carry back in your hand; peradventure it was an oversight;

Also your brother take along, and arise, go again unto the man.

And may God the Almighty give you mercy before the man,. that he may send away to you your other brother, and Benjamin. And I, if I am to be bereaved, let me be bereaved.

And the men took that present ; and twofold money they took in their hand, as also Benjamin; and they rose up, and went down to Egypt, and stood before Joseph.

And when Joseph saw Benjamin with them, he said to the superintendent of his house, Bring these men into the house, and slay, and make ready; for with me shall these men dine at noon.

And the man did as Joseph had said ; and the man brought the men into Joseph's house.

And the men were afraid, because they were

brought into Joseph's house: and they said, Because of the money that came back in our sacks at the first time are we brought in; that he may seek occasion against us, and take us for bondmen, together with our asses.

And they came near to the man who was appointed over Joseph's house, and they spoke with him at the door of the house,

And they said, Pardon, my lord, we came down at the first time to buy food :

And it came to pass, when we came to the inn, that we opened our sacks, and, behold, every man's money was in the mouth of his sack, our money in its full weight ; and we have brought it back in our hand.

And other money have we brought down in our hand to buy food ; we know not who hath put our money in our sacks.

And he said, Peace be to you, fear not ; your God, and the God of your father, hath given you a treasure in your sacks; your money hath come to me. And he brought Simeon out unto them.

And the man brought the men into Joseph's house ; and he gave them water, and they washed their feet, and he gave provender to their asses.

And they made ready the present before Joseph came home at noon ; for they had heard that they should eat bread there.

And when Joseph came home, they brought him the present which was in their hand into the house, and bowed themselves to him to the earth.

And he asked them after their welfare, and said,

Is your old father well, of whom ye spoke? Is he yet alive?

And they answered, Thy servant, our father, is in good health, he is yet alive. And they bowed down their heads, and prostrated themselves.

And he lifted up his eyes, and saw his brother Benjamin, his mother's son, and said, Is this your youngest brother of whom ye spoke unto me? And he said, God be gracious unto thee, my son.

And Joseph hastened away, for his affection toward his brother became enkindled, and he sought to weep; and he entered into his chamber, and wept there.

And he washed his face, and came out, and refrained himself, and said, Set on the bread.

. . . .

And he commanded the superintendent of his house, saying, Fill the sacks of these men with food, as much as they can carry, and put every man's money in the mouth of his sack.

And my cup, the silver cup, thou shalt put in the mouth of the sack of the youngest, and the money for his corn. And he did according to the word of Joseph which he had spoken.

As soon as the morning was light, the men were sent away, they and their asses.

They were gone out of the city, not yet far off, when Joseph said unto the superintendent of his house, Up, follow after the men; and when thou hast overtaken them, say unto them, Wherefore have ye returned evil for good?

Is not this out of which my lord drinketh, and

whereby he divineth? ye have done evil in so doing.

And he overtook them, and he spoke unto them these same words.

And they said unto him, Wherefore will my lord speak such words as these? God forbid that thy servants should do any thing like this.

Behold the money, which we found in the mouth of our sacks, we brought back unto thee out of the land of Canaan: how then should we steal out of thy lord's house silver or gold?

With whomsoever of thy servants it be found, let him die; and we also will be bondmen unto my lord.

And he said, Now also let it be according to your words: he with whom it is found shall be my servant: but ye shall be blameless.

And they made haste, and every one of them took down his sack to the ground, and every one opened his sack.

And he searched, at the eldest he began, and at the youngest he left off; and the cup was found in Benjamin's sack.

Then they rent their clothes, and every one loaded his ass and they returned to the city.

And Judah and his brothers came into Joseph's house, and he was yet there; and they fell down before him to the ground.

And Joseph said unto them, What deed is this that ye have done? knew ye not that such a man as I can certainly divine?

And Judah said, What shall we say unto my

lord? What shall we speak? or how shall we justify ourselves? God hath found out the iniquity of thy servants: behold we are servants unto my lord, both we, as also he in whose hand the cup was found.

And he said, God forbid that I should do this: the man in whose hand the cup was found, he shall be my servant; and as for you, go you up in peace unto your father.

BIBLE—LEESER'S TRANSLATION

21

JOSEPH AND HIS BRETHREN

Genesis xliv. 18-34; xlv. 1-3, 14-15, 17-18; xlvi. 29-30.

Then Judah came near unto him, and said, Pardon, my lord, let thy servant, I pray thee, speak a word into my lord's ears, and let not thy anger burn against thy servant; for thou art even as Pharaoh.

My lord asked his servants, saying, Have ye a father, or a brother?

And we said unto my lord, We have an old father, and a little child, born in his old age; and his brother is dead, and he alone is left of his mother, and his father loveth him.

And thou saidst unto thy servants, Bring him down unto me, that I may set my eye upon him.

And we said unto my lord, The lad cannot leave his father: for if he should leave his father, he would die.

And thou saidst unto thy servants, Except your youngest brother come down with you, ye shall not see my face any more.

And it came to pass, when we came up unto thy servant my father, that we told him the words of my lord.

And our father said, Go back, and buy us a little food.

And we said, we cannot go down : if our youngest brother be with us, then will we go down ; for we cannot see the man's face, except our youngest brother be with us.

And thy servant my father said unto us, Ye know that my wife bore me two sons ;

And the one went out from me, and I said, Surely he hath been torn in pieces ; and I have not seen him up to this time.

And if ye take this one also from me, and mischief befall him, ye will bring down my gray hairs with sorrow to the grave.

And, now, when I come to thy servant my father, and the lad be not with us; seeing that his life is bound up in the lad's life ;

It will come to pass, that when he seeth that the lad is not with us, he will die : and thy servants would thus bring down the gray hairs of thy servant our father with sorrow to the grave.

For thy servant became surety for the lad unto my father, saying, If I bring him not unto thee, then shall I have sinned against my father all the days.

Now therefore, I pray thee, let thy servant abide

instead of the lad as bondman to my lord ; and let the lad go up with his brothers.

For how shall I go up to my father, and the lad be not with me? I should perhaps be compelled to witness the evil which would come on my father.

Then could Joseph not restrain himself before all those that stood by him ; and he cried, Cause every man to go out from me. And there remained no man with him, while Joseph made himself known unto his brothers.

And he raised his voice in weeping ; and the Egyptians heard it, and the house of Pharaoh heard it.

And Joseph said unto his brothers, I am Joseph; doth my father yet live?

. . . .

And he fell upon his brother Benjamin's neck, and wept ; and Benjamin wept upon his neck.

And he kissed all his brothers, and wept upon them ; and after that his brothers spoke with him.

. . . .

And Pharaoh said unto Joseph, Say unto thy brothers, This do ye : load your beasts, and go, get you unto the land of Canaan ;

And take your father and your households, and come unto me ; and I will give you the best of the land of Egypt, and ye shall eat the fat of the land.

. . . .

And Joseph made ready his chariot, and went up to meet Israel his father, to Goshen ; and when he obtained sight of him, he fell on his neck, and wept on his neck a good while.

And Israel said unto Joseph, Let me die now, since I have seen thy face, that thou art yet alive.

BIBLE—LEESER'S TRANSLATION

22

PASSAGE OF THE RED SEA

'Mid the light spray their snorting camels stood,
Nor bathed a fetlock in the nauseous flood—
He comes—their leader comes!—the man of God
O'er the wide waters lifts his mighty rod,
And onward treads—the circling waves retreat
In hoarse deep murmurs, from his holy feet;
And the chased surges, inly roaring, show
The hard wet sand and coral hills below.
With limbs that falter, and with hearts that swell,
Down, down they pass—a steep and slippery dell.
Around them rise in pristine chaos hurled,
The ancient rocks, the secrets of the world;
And flowers that blush beneath the ocean green,
And caves, the sea-calves' low-roofed haunt, are seen.
Down, safely down the narrow pass they tread;
The beetling waters storm above their head:
While far behind retires the sinking day,
And fades on Edom's hills its latest ray.
Yet not from Israel fled the friendly light,
Or dark to them, or cheerless came the night,

Still in their van, along the dreadful road,
Blazed broad and fierce the brandished torch of
    God.
Its meteor glare a tenfold lustre gave
On the long mirror of the rosy wave:
While its blest beams a sunlike heat supply,
Warm every cheek, and dance in every eye—
To them alone—for Mizraim's wizard train
Invoke for light their monster-gods in vain:
Clouds heaped on clouds their struggling sight
    confine,
And tenfold darkness broods above their line.
Yet on they fare, by reckless vengeance led,
And range unconscious through the ocean's bed.
Till midway now—that strange and fiery form
Showed his dread visage lightning through the
    storm;
With withering splendor blasted all their might,
And brake their chariot-wheels, and marred their
    coursers' flight. . . . .
"Fly, Mizraim, fly!"—From Edom's coral strand
Again the prophet stretched his dreadful wand:—
With one wild crash the thundering waters sweep,
And all is waves—a dark and lonely deep.

REGINALD HEBER

23

SONG OF MOSES

Exodus xv. 1-18.

Then sang Moses and the children of Israel this song unto the Lord, and spake, saying,

I will sing unto the Lord, for he hath triumphed
   gloriously:
The horse and his rider hath he thrown into the
   sea.
The Lord is my strength and song,
And he is become my salvation:
This is my God, and I will praise him;
My father's God, and I will exalt him.
The Lord is a man of war:
The Lord is his name.
Pharaoh's chariots and his host hath he cast into
   the sea:
And his chosen captains are sunk in the Red Sea.
The deeps cover them:
They went down into the depths like a stone.
Thy right hand, O Lord, is glorious in power,
Thy right hand, O Lord, dasheth in pieces the
   enemy.
And in the greatness of thine excellency thou over-
   throwest them that rise up against thee:
Thou sendest forth thy wrath, it consumeth them
   as stubble.
And with the blast of thy nostrils the waters were
   piled up,
The floods stood upright as an heap;
The deeps were congealed in the heart of the sea.
The enemy said,
I will pursue, I will overtake, I will divide the spoil:
My lust shall be satisfied upon them:
I will draw my sword, my hand shall destroy them.
Thou didst blow with thy wind, the sea covered
   them:

They sank as lead in the mighty waters.
Who is like unto thee, O Lord, among the gods?
Who is like thee, glorious in holiness,
Fearful in praises, doing wonders?
Thou stretchedst out thy right hand,
The earth swallowed them.
Thou in thy mercy hast led the people which thou
    hast redeemed :
Thou hast guided them in thy strength to thy holy
    habitation.
The peoples have heard, they tremble :
Pangs have taken hold on the inhabitants of Phil-
    istia.
Then were the dukes of Edom amazed ;
The mighty men of Moab, trembling taketh hold
    upon them :
All the inhabitants of Canaan are melted away..
Terror and dread falleth upon them ;
By the greatness of thine arm they are as still as a
    stone ;
Till thy people pass over, O Lord,
Till the people pass over which thou hast purchased.
Thou shalt bring them in, and plant them in the
    mountain of thine inheritance,
The place, O Lord, which thou hast made for thee
    to dwell in,
The sanctuary, O Lord, which thy hands have es-
    tablished.
The Lord shall reign for ever and ever.

                BIBLE—REVISED VERSION

24

MOUNT HOR

Numbers xx. 23-29.

They have left the camp, with its tents outspreading,
  Like a garden of lilies, on Edom's plain ;
They are climbing the mountain, in silence treading
  A path which *one* shall not tread again.
Two aged brothers the way are leading,
  There follows a youth in the solemn train.

O'er a sister's bier they have just been bending ;
  The desert prophetess sleeps hard by :
With her toilsome sojourn nearly ending,
  With Judah's mountains before her eye,
The echoes of Kadesh and Canaan blending,
  She has calmly turned her aside to die !

They come, not to gaze on the matchless glory,
  On grandeur the like of which earth has not ;
A billowy ocean of mountains hoary,
  A chaos of cliffs round this awful spot ;
A vision like that in some old-world story,
  Too terrible ever to be forgot.

. . . .

The king and the priest move on unspeaking,
  The desert-priest and the desert-king ;
'Tis a grave, a mountain-grave they are seeking,
  Fit end of a great life-wandering !
And here, till the day of the glory-streaking,
  This desert-eagle must fold his wing.

The fetters of age have but lightly bound him,
 This bold sharp steep he can bravely breast;
With his six-score wondrous years around him,
 He climbs like youth to the mountain's crest.
The mortal moment at last has found him,
 Willing to tarry, yet glad to rest.

Is that a tear-drop his dim eye leaving,
 As he looks his last on yon desert-sun?
Is that a sigh his faint bosom heaving,
 As he lays his ephod in silence down?
'Twas a passing mist, to his sky still cleaving; —
 But the sky has brightened,—the cloud is gone!

In his shroud of rock they have gently wound him,
 'Tis a Bethel-pillow that love has given;
I see no gloom of the grave around him,
 The death-bed fetters have all been riven;
'Tis the angel of life, not of death, that has found him,
 And this is to him the gate of heaven.

He has seen the tombs of old Mizraim's wonder,
 Where the haughty Pharaohs embalm'd recline;
But no pyramid-tomb, with its costly grandeur,
 Can once be compared with this mountain-shrine;
No monarch of Memphis is swathed in splendor,
 High Priest of the desert, like this of thine!

Not with thy nation thy bones are lying,
 Nor Israel's hills shall thy burial see;
Yet with Edom's vultures around thee flying,
 Safe and unrifled thy dust shall be;—

Oh who would not covet so calm a dying,
    And who would not rest by the side of thee?

Not with thy fathers thy slumber tasting;
    From sister and brother thou seem'st to flee.
Not in Shechem's plain are thy ashes wasting,
    Not in Machpelah thy grave shall be;
In the land of the stranger thy dust is resting,—
    Yet who would not sleep by the side of thee?

Alone and safe, in the happy keeping
    Of rocks and sands, till the glorious morn,
They have laid thee down for thy lonely sleeping,
    Waysore and weary and labor-worn;
While faintly the sound of a nation's weeping
    From the vale beneath thee is upward borne.

   .   .   .   .

Alone and safe, in the holy keeping
    Of Him who holdeth the grave's cold key,
They have laid thee down for the blessed sleeping,
    The quiet rest which his dear ones see;—
And why o'er thee should *we* weep the weeping,
    For who would not rest by the side of thee?

Three Hebrew cradles, the Nile-palms under,
    Rocked three sweet babes upon Egypt's plain;
Three desert-graves must these dear ones sunder;
    Three sorrowful links of a broken chain;
Kadesh and Hor, and Nebo yonder,—
    Three way-marks now for the pilgrim-train.

Are these my way-marks, these tombs of ages?
    Are these my guides to the land of rest?

Are these grim rock-tombs the stony pages,
　　Which show how to follow the holy blest?
And bid me rise, 'bove each storm that rages,
　　Like a weary dove to its olive nest?

　　.　.　.　.　.　.　.　.　.

On this rugged cliff, while the sun is dying
　　Behind yon majestic mountain-wall,
I stand;—not a cloudlet above me flying,—
　　Not a foot is stirring, no voices call;—
A traveller lonely, a stranger, trying
　　To muse o'er this wondrous funeral.

In silence we stand, till the faint stars cover
　　This grave of ages. Yes, thus would we
Still look and linger, and gaze and hover
　　About this cave where thy dust may be!
Great Priest of the desert, thy toil is over,
　　And who would not rest by the side of thee?

　　.　.　.　.　.　.　.　.　.

The night of ages bends softly o'er us;
　　Four thousand autumns have well-nigh fled,
Love watches still the old tomb before us
　　Of sainted dust, in its mountain-bed;
Till the longed-for trump shall awake the chorus
　　From desert and field, of the blessed dead.

　　　　　　　　　　HORATIUS BONAR

25
BURIAL OF MOSES

And he buried him in a valley in the land of Moab, over against Beth-peor: but no man knoweth of his sepulchre unto this day.—DEUT. xxxiv. 6.

By Nebo's lonely mountain,
  On this side Jordan's wave,
In a vale in the land of Moab,
  There lies a lonely grave;
But no man built that sepulchre,
  And no man saw it e'er,
For the angels of God upturned the sod,
  And laid the dead man there.

That was the grandest funeral
  That ever passed on earth;
Yet no man heard the trampling,
  Or saw the train go forth;
Noiselessly as the daylight
  Comes when the night is done,
And the crimson streak on ocean's cheek
  Grows into the great sun,—

Noiselessly as the spring-time
  Her crown of verdure weaves,
And all the trees on all the hills
  Unfold their thousand leaves,—
So, without sound of music,
  Or voice of them that wept,
Silently down from the mountain's crown
  The great procession swept.

. . . .

Lo! when the warrior dieth,
  His comrades in the war,
With arms reversed, and muffled drums,
  Follow the funeral car.
They show the banners taken,
  They tell his battles won,
And after him lead his masterless steed,
  While peals the minute-gun.

Amid the noblest of the land
  Men lay the sage to rest,
And give the bard an honored place,
  With costly marbles dressed,
In the great minster transept,
  Where lights like glories fall,
And the sweet choir sings, and the organ rings
  Along the emblazoned hall.

This was the bravest warrior
  That ever buckled sword;
This the most gifted poet
  That ever breathed a word;
And never earth's philosopher
  Traced, with his golden pen,
On the deathless page, truths half so sage
  As *he* wrote down for men.

And had he not high honor?
  The hill-side for a pall;
To lie in state while angels wait,
  With stars for tapers tall;
And the dark rock-pines like tossing plumes,
  Over his bier to wave;

And God's own hand, in that lonely land,
  To lay him in his grave!—
. . . .
O lonely tomb in Moab's land!
  O dark Beth-peor's hill!
Speak to these curious hearts of ours,
  And teach them to be still.
God hath his mysteries of grace,—
  Ways that we cannot tell;
He hides them deep, like the secret sleep
  Of him he loved so well.

C. F. ALEXANDER

26

WEEP, CHILDREN OF ISRAEL

Weep, weep for him, the Man of God—
  In yonder vale he sunk to rest;
But none of earth can point the sod
  That flowers above his sacred breast.
Weep, children of Israel, weep!

His doctrine fell like heaven's rain,
  His words refreshed like heaven's dew—
Oh, ne'er shall Israel see again
  A chief, to God and her so true.
Weep, children of Israel, weep!

Remember ye his parting gaze,
  His farewell song by Jordan's tide,
When, full of glory and of days,
  He saw the promised land—and died.
Weep, children of Israel, weep!

Yet died he not as men who sink,
  Before our eyes, to soulless clay:
But, changed to spirit, like a wink
  Of summer lightning, pass'd away.
Weep, children of Israel, weep!

THOMAS MOORE

27

"NO MAN KNOWETH OF HIS SEPULCHRE"

When he who, from the scourge of wrong,
  Aroused the Hebrew tribes to fly,
Saw the fair region, promised long,
  And bowed him on the hills to die,

God made his grave to men unknown,
  Where Moab's rocks a vale infold,
And laid the aged seer alone,
  To slumber while the world grows old.

Thus still, whene'er the good and just
  Close the dim eyes on life and pain,
Heaven watches o'er their slumbering dust
  Till the pure spirit comes again.

Though nameless, tramped and forgot,
  His servant's humble ashes lie,
Yet God has marked and sealed the spot,
  To call its inmate to the sky.

WILLIAM CULLEN BRYANT

28

DEBORAH'S SONG
Judges v. 1-31.

Then sang Deborah and Barak the son of Abi-
noam on that day, saying,
For that the leaders took the lead in Israel,
For that the people offered themselves willingly,
Bless ye the Lord.
Hear, O ye kings; give ear, O ye princes;
I, even I, will sing unto the Lord;
I will sing praise to the Lord, the God of Israel.
Lord, when thou wentest forth out of Seir,
When thou marchedst out of the field of Edom,
The earth trembled, the heavens also dropped,
Yea, the clouds dropped water.
The mountains flowed down at the presence of the
 Lord,
Even yon Sinai at the presence of the Lord, the
 God of Israel.
In the days of Shamgar the son of Anath,
In the days of Jael, the highways were unoccupied,
And the travellers walked through byways.
The rulers ceased in Israel, they ceased,
Until that I Deborah arose,
That I arose a mother in Israel.
They chose new gods;
Then was war in the gates:
Was there a shield or spear seen
Among forty thousand in Israel?
My heart is toward the governors of Israel,

That offered themselves willingly among the people;
Bless ye the Lord.
Tell of it, ye that ride on white asses,
Ye that sit on rich carpets,
And ye that walk by the way.
Far from the noise of archers, in the places of drawing water,
There shall they rehearse the righteous acts of the Lord,
Even the righteous acts of his rule in Israel,
Then the people of the Lord went down to the gates.
Awake, awake, Deborah;
Awake, awake, utter a song:
Arise, Barak, and lead thy captivity
Captive, thou son of Abinoam.
Then came down a remnant of the nobles and the people;
The Lord came down for me against the mighty.
Out of Ephraim came down they whose root is in Amalek;
After thee, Benjamin, among thy peoples:
Out of Machir came down governors,
And out of Zebulun they that handle the marshal's staff.
And the princes of Issachar were with Deborah;
As was Issachar, so was Barak;
Into the valley they rushed forth at his feet.
By the water courses of Reuben
There were great resolves of heart.
Why satest thou among the sheepfolds,
To hear the pipings for the flocks?

At the watercourses of Reuben
There were great searchings of heart.
Gilead abode beyond Jordan;
And Dan, why did he remain in ships?
Asher sat still at the haven of the sea,
And abode by his creeks.
Zebulun was a people that jeoparded their lives
    unto the death,
And Naphtali upon the high places of the field.
The kings came and fought;
Then fought the kings of Canaan,
In Taanach by the waters of Megiddo:
They took no gain of money.
They fought from heaven,
The stars in their courses fought against Sisera.
The river Kishon swept them away,
That ancient river, the river Kishon.
O my soul, march on with strength.
Then did the horsehoofs stamp
By reason of the pransings, the pransing of their
    strong ones.
Curse ye Meroz, said the angel of the Lord,
Curse ye bitterly the inhabitants thereof:
Because they came not to the help of the Lord,
To the help of the Lord against the mighty.
Blessed above women shall Jael be,
The wife of Heber the Kenite,
Blessed shall she be above women in the tent.
He asked water and she gave him milk:
She brought him butter in a lordly dish.
She put her hand to the nail,
And her right hand to the workmen's hammer,

And with the hammer she smote Sisera, she smote
 through his head,
Yea, she pierced and struck through his temples.
At her feet he bowed, he fell, he lay :
At her feet he bowed, he fell :
Where he bowed, there he fell down dead.
Through the window she looked forth, and cried,
The mother of Sisera cried through the lattice,
Why is his chariot so long in coming?
Why tarry the wheels of his chariots?
Her wise ladies answered her,
Yea, she returned answer to herself,
Have they not found, have they not divided the
 spoil?
A damsel, two damsels to every man ;
To Sisera a spoil of divers colors,
A spoil of divers colors of embroidery,
Of divers colors of embroidery on both sides, on
 the necks of the spoil ?
So let all thine enemies perish, O Lord :
But let them that love him be as the sun when he
 goeth forth in his might.

BIBLE—REVISED VERSION

29

THE WIFE OF MANOAH TO HER HUSBAND

Against the sunset's glowing wall
The city towers rise black and tall,
Where Zorah, on its rocky height,
Stands like an armed man in the light.

Down Eshtaol's vales of ripened grain
Falls like a cloud the night amain,
And up the hillsides climbing slow
The barley reapers homeward go.

Look, dearest, how our fair child's head
The sunset light hath hallowèd,
Where at this olive's foot he lies,
Uplooking to the tranquil skies.

Oh, while beneath the fervent heat
Thy sickle swept the bearded wheat,
I've watched, with mingled joy and dread,
Our child upon his grassy bed.

Joy, which the mother feels alone
Whose morning hope like mine had flown,
When to her bosom, over-blessed,
A dearer life than hers is pressed.

Dread, for the future dark and still,
Which shapes our dear one to its will;
Forever in his large, calm eyes,
I read a tale of sacrifice.

The same foreboding awe I felt
When at the altar's side we knelt,
And he, who as a pilgrim came,
Rose, winged and glorious, through the flame.

I slept not, though the wild bees made
A dreamlike murmuring in the shade,
And on me the warm-fingered hours
Pressed with the drowsy smell of flowers.

Before me, in a vision, rose
The hosts of Israel's scornful foes,—
Rank over rank, helm, shield and spear,
Glittered in noon's hot atmosphere.

I heard their boast, and bitter word,
Their mockery of the Hebrew's Lord,
I saw their hands his ark assail,
Their feet profane his holy veil.

No angel down the blue space spoke,
No thunder from the still sky broke;
But in their midst, in power and awe
Like God's waked wrath, our child I saw!

A child no more!—harsh-browed and strong,
He towered a giant in the throng,
And down his shoulders, broad and bare,
Swept the black terror of his hair.

He raised his arm—he smote amain;
As round the reaper falls the grain,
So the dark host around him fell,
So sank the foes of Israel!

Again I looked. In sunlight shone
The towers and domes of Askelon.
Priest, warrior, slave, a mighty crowd,
Within her idol temple bowed.

Yet one knelt not; stark, gaunt, and blind,
His arms the massive pillars twined,—
An eyeless captive, strong with hate,
He stood there like an evil Fate.

The red shrines smoked,—the trumpets pealed:
He stooped,—the giant columns reeled;
Reeled tower and fane, sank arch and wall,
And the thick dust-cloud closed o'er all!

Above the shriek, the crash, the groan
Of the fallen pride of Askelon,
I heard, sheer down the echoing sky,
A voice as of an angel cry,—

The voice of him, who at our side
Sat through the golden eventide;
Of him who, on thy altar's blaze
Rose fire-winged, with his song of praise.

"Rejoice o'er Israel's broken chain,
Gray mother of the mighty slain!
Rejoice!" it cried, "he vanquisheth!
The strong in life is strong in death!

"To him shall Zorah's daughters raise
Through coming years their hymns of praise,
And gray old men at evening tell
Of all he wrought for Israel.

"And they who sing and they who hear
Alike shall hold thy memory dear,
And pour their blessings on thy head,
O mother of the mighty dead!"

It ceased; and though a sound I heard
As if great wings the still air stirred,
I only saw the barley sheaves
And hill half hid by olive leaves.

I bowed my face, in awe and fear,
On the dear child who slumbered near;
" With me, as with my only son,
O God," I said, "Thy will be done!"

JOHN GREENLEAF WHITTIER

30

DEATH OF SAMSON

(From *Samson Agonistes*)

The building was a spacious theatre,
Half round on two main pillars vaulted high,
With seats where all the lords, and each degree
Of sort, might sit in order to behold;
The other side was open, where the throng
On banks and scaffolds under sky might stand:
I among these aloof obscurely stood.
The feast and noon grew high, and sacrifice
Had filled their hearts with mirth, high cheer, and
  wine,
When to their sports they turned. Immediately
Was Samson as a public servant brought,
In their state livery clad: before him pipes
And timbrels; on each side went armed guards;
Both horse and foot, before him and behind,
Archers and slingers, cataphracts and spears.
At sight of him the people with a shout
Rifted the air, clamoring their god with praise,
Who had made their dreadful enemy their thrall.
He patient, but undaunted, where they led him,

Came to the place; and what was set before him,
Which without help of eye might be assayed,
To heave, pull, draw, or break, he still performed
All with incredible, stupendous force,
None daring to appear antagonist.
At length, for intermission sake, they led him
Between the pillars; he his guide requested
(For so from such as nearer stood we heard)
As over-tired to let him lean awhile
With both his arms on those two massy pillars,
That to the arched roof gave main support.
He, unsuspicious, led him; which when Samson
Felt in his arms, with head awhile inclined,
And eyes fast fixed, he stood, as one who prayed,
Or some great matter in his mind revolved:
At last, with head erect, thus cried aloud:—
"Hitherto, Lords, what your commands imposed
I have performed, as reason was, obeying,
Not without wonder or delight beheld;
Now, of my own accord, such other trial
I mean to show you of my strength yet greater
As with amaze shall strike all who behold."
This uttered, straining all his nerves he bowed;
As with the force of winds and waters pent,
When mountains tremble, those two massy pillars
With horrible convulsion to and fro
He tugged, he shook, till down they came, and
  drew
The whole roof after them with burst of thunder
Upon the heads of all who sat beneath,
Lords, ladies, captains, counsellors, or priests,
Their choice nobility and flower, not only

Of this but each Philistian city round,
Met from all parts to solemnize this feast.
Samson, with these inmixed, inevitably
Pulled down the same destruction on himself;
The vulgar only scaped who stood without.

JOHN MILTON

31

RUTH

She stood breast-high amid the corn,
Clasped by the golden light of morn,
Like the sweetheart of the sun,
Who many a glowing kiss had won.

On her cheek an autumn flush
Deeply ripened;—such a blush
In the midst of brown was born,
Like red poppies grown with corn.

Round her eyes her tresses fell,—
Which were blackest none could tell;
But long lashes veiled a light,
That had else been all too bright.

And her hat, with shady brim,
Made her tressy forehead dim;—
Thus she stood amid the stooks,
Praising God with sweetest looks:—

Sure, I said, heav'n did not mean
Where I reap thou shouldst but glean·
Lay thy sheaf adown and come,
Share my harvest and my home.

THOMAS HOOD

32

THE CHILD SAMUEL

1 Samuel iii. 1-15.

Hushed was the evening hymn,
The temple courts were dark;
The lamp was burning dim
Before the sacred Ark,
When suddenly a voice divine
Rang through the silence of the shrine.

The old man meek and mild,
The priest of Israel slept;
His watch the temple child,
The little Levite kept;
And what from Eli's sense was sealed,
The Lord to Hannah's son revealed.

O give me Samuel's ear,
The open ear, O Lord,
Alive and quick to hear
Each whisper of Thy word;
Like him to answer at Thy call,
And so obey Thee first of all.

O give me Samuel's heart,
A lowly heart that waits,
Where in Thy house Thou art,
Or watches at Thy gates;
By day and night, a heart that still
Moves at the breathing of Thy will.

O give me Samuel's mind,
O sweet, unmurmuring faith,
Obedient and resigned
To Thee in life and death;
That I may read with child-like eyes,
Truths that are hidden from the wise.

J. D. BORTHWICK

33

SAUL

(Extract)

Said Abner, "At last thou art come!
  Ere I tell, ere thou speak,
Kiss my cheek, wish me well!" Then I wished it,
  And did kiss his cheek.
And he: "Since the king, O my friend,
  For thy countenance sent,
Nor drunken nor eaten have we;
  Nor until from his tent
Thou return with the joyful assurance
  The king liveth yet,
Shall our lip with the honey be brightened,
  —The water be wet.

"For out of the black mid-tent's silence,
  A space of three days,
No sound hath escaped to thy servants,
  Of prayer nor of praise,
To betoken that Saul and the Spirit
  Have ended their strife,
And that faint in his triumph the monarch
  Sinks back upon life.

"Yet now my heart leaps, O beloved!
   God's child, with his dew
On thy gracious gold hair, and those lilies
   Still living and blue
As thou brak'st them to twine round thy harp-
    strings,
   As if no wild heat
Were raging to torture the desert!"
   Then I, as was meet,
Knelt down to the God of my fathers,
   And rose on my feet,
And ran o'er the sand burnt to powder.
   The tent was unlooped;
I pulled up the spear that obstructed,
   And under I stooped;
Hands and knees on the slippery grass-patch—
   All withered and gone—
That leads to the second enclosure,
   I groped my way on,
Till I felt where the foldskirts fly open;
   Then once more I prayed,
And opened the foldskirts and entered,
   And was not afraid;
And spoke, "Here is David, thy servant!"
   And no voice replied;
And first I saw naught but the blackness;
   But soon I descried
A something more black than the blackness
   —The vast, the upright
Main-prop which sustains the pavilion,—
   And slow into sight

Grew a figure, gigantic, against it,
  And blackest of all;—
Then a sunbeam that burst thro' the tent-roof,—
  Showed Saul.
He stood as erect as that tent-prop;
  Both arms stretched out wide
On the great cross-support in the centre
  That goes to each side:
So he bent not a muscle, but hung there
  As, caught in his pangs
And waiting his change, the king-serpent
  All heavily hangs,
Far away from his kind, in the pine,
  Till deliverance come
With the spring-time,—so agonized Saul,
  Drear and stark, blind and dumb.
Then I tuned my harp—took off the lilies
  We twine round its chords
Lest they snap 'neath the stress of the noontide
  —Those sunbeams like swords!
And I first played the tune all our sheep know,
  As, one after one,
So docile they come to the pen-door
  Till folding be done;
—They are white and untorn by the bushes,
  For lo, they have fed
Where the long grasses stifle the water
  Within the stream's bed:
How one after one seeks its lodging,
  As star follows star
Into eve and the blue far above us,
  —So blue and so far!

Then the tune for which quails on the cornland
 Will leave each his mate
To follow the player; then what makes
 The crickets elate,
Till for boldness they fight one another:
 And then, what has weight
To set the quick jerboa a-musing
 Outside his sand house
—There are none such as he for a wonder—
 Half bird and half mouse!
—God made all the creatures and gave them
 Our love and our fear,
To show, we and they are his children,
 One family here.
Then I played the help-tune of our reapers,
 Their wine-song, when hand
Grasps hand, eye lights eye in good friendship,
 And great hearts expand,
And grow one in the sense of this world's life;
 And then, the low song
When the dead man is praised on his journey—
 "Bear, bear him along
With his few faults shut up like dead flowrets;
 Are balm-seeds not here
To console us? The land is left none such
 As he on the bier—
Oh, would we might keep thee, my brother!"
 And then, the glad chant
Of the marriage,—first go the young maidens,
 Next, she whom we vaunt
As the beauty, the pride of our dwelling:

And then the great march
When man runs to man to assist him,
  And buttress and arch
Naught can break . . . who shall harm them,
  our friends?
  Then the chorus intoned
As the Levites go up to the altar
  In glory enthroned—
But I stopped here—for here in the darkness,
  Saul groaned.
And I paused, held my breath in such silence!
  And listened apart;
And the tent shook, for mighty Saul shuddered,—
  And sparkles 'gan dart
From the jewels that woke in his turban
  —At once with a start
All its lordly male sapphires, and rubies
  Courageous at heart;
So the head—but the body still moved not,
  Still hung there erect.
And I bent once again to my playing,
  Pursued it unchecked,
As I sang, "Oh, our manhood's prime vigor!
  —No spirit feels waste,
No muscle is stopped in its playing,
  No sinew unbraced;—
And the wild joys of living! The leaping
  From rock up to rock—
The rending their boughs from the palm-trees,—
  The cool silver shock
Of a plunge in the pool's living water—
  The haunt of the bear,

And the sultriness showing the lion
    Is couched in his lair:
And the meal—the rich dates—yellowed over
    With gold dust divine,
And the locust's flesh steeped in the pitcher,
    The full draught of wine,
And the sleep in the dried river channel
    Where tall rushes tell
The water was wont to go warbling
    So softly and well,—
How good is man's life here, mere living!
    How fit to employ
The heart and the soul and the senses for ever in joy!
Hast thou loved the white locks of thy father
    Whose sword thou didst guard
When he trusted thee forth to the wolf hunt
    For glorious reward?
Didst thou see the thin hands of thy mother
    Held up, as men sung
The song of the nearly-departed,
    And heard her faint tongue
Joining in while it could to the witness,
    'Let one more attest
I have lived, seen God's hand thro' that lifetime,
    And all was for best . . .'
Then they sang thro' their tears, in strong triumph,
    Not much—but the rest!
And thy brothers—the help and the contest,
    The working whence grew
Such result, as from seething grape-bundles
    The spirit so true:

And the friends of thy boyhood—that boyhood
　With wonder and hope,
Present promise, and wealth in the future,—
　The eye's eagle scope,—
Till lo, thou art grown to a monarch,
　A people is thine!
Oh all gifts the world offers singly,
　On one head combine,
On one head the joy and the pride,
　Even rage like the throe
That opes the rock, helps its glad labor,
　And lets the gold go—
And ambition that sees a sun lead it—
　Oh, all of these—all
Combine to unite in one creature
　—Saul!"

ROBERT BROWNING

34

THE WATER OF BETHLEHEM GATE

(From *Three Cups of Cold Water*)

The princely David, with his outlaw band,
Lodged in the cave Adullam. Wild and fierce,
With lion-like faces, and with eagle eyes,
They followed where he led. The danger pressed,
For over all the land the Philistines
Had spread their armies. Through Rephaim's vale
Their dark tents mustered thick, and David's home,
His father's city, Bethlehem, owned them lords.
'Twas harvest, and the crops of ripening corn

They ravaged, and with rude feet trampled down
The tender vines. Men hid themselves for fear
In wood or caves. The brave undaunted few,
Gathering round David, sought the mountain hold.
The sun was hot, and all day long they watched
With spear in hand and never-resting eye,
As those who wait for battle. But at eve
The eye grew dim, the lips were parched with thirst,
And from that arid rock no trickling stream
Of living water gushed. From time-worn skins
The tainted drops were poured, and fevered lips
Half-loathing drank them up. And David's soul
Was weary; the hot simoon scorched his veins;
The strong sun smote on him, and, faint and sick,
He sat beneath the shadow of the rock.
And then before his eyes a vision came,
Cool evening, meadows green, and pleasant sounds
Of murmuring fountains. Oft in days of youth,
When leading home his flocks as sunset fell,
That fount had quenched his thirst, and dark-eyed
  girls,
The pride and joy of Bethlehem, meeting there,
Greeted the shepherd boy, their chieftain's son
(As, bright and fair with waving locks of gold
Exulting in the flush of youth's full glow,
He mingled with their throng), and gazing, rapt
With wonder at his beauty, gave him drink.
And now the words came feebly from his lips,
A murmur half in silence, which the ear
Of faithful followers caught : " Oh ! who will bring
From that fair stream, which flowing by the gate
Of Bethlehem's wall makes music in the ear,

One drop to cool this tongue?" They heard, the
    three,
The mightiest of the thirty, swift of foot
As are the harts upon the mountains, strong
As are the lions down by Jordan's banks;
They heard and darted forth; down rock and crag
They leapt, as leaps the torrent on its course,
Through plain and vale they sped, and never stayed,
Until the wide encampment of the foe
Warned them of danger nigh. But not for fear
Abandoned they their task. When evening fell,
And all the Philistines were hushed in sleep,
And over all the plain the full bright moon
Poured its rich lustre, onward still they stole,
By tent fires creeping with hushed breath, and feet
That feared to wake the echoes, till at last
They heard the babbling music, and the gleam
Of rippling moonlight caught their eager eye,
And o'er them fell the shade of Bethlehem's gate.
They tarried not. One full delicious draught
Slaked their fierce thirst, and then with anxious
    haste
They filled their water-urn, and full of joy,
They bore it back in triumph to their lord.
With quickened steps they tracked their path again
O'er plain and valley, up o'er rock and crag,
And as the early sunlight kissed the hills
They stood before him. He had won their hearts
By brave deeds, gentle words, and stainless life,
And now they came to give him proof of love,
And pouring out the water bade him drink.
But lo! he would not taste. He heard their tale

(In few words told, as brave men tell their deeds),
And lifting up his hands with solemn prayer,
As though he stood, a priest, before the shrine,
He poured it on the earth before the Lord.
"Far be it from me, God, that I should drink,
The slave of selfish lust, forgetting Thee,
Forgetting these my brothers. In Thine eyes
This water fresh and cool is as the blood
Of hero-souls who jeoparded their lives.
That blood I may not taste. . . To Thee, O Lord,
To Thee I pour it. Thou wilt pardon me
For mine unkingly weakness, pardon them
For all rough deeds of war. Their noble love
Shall cover all their sins ; for Thou hast claimed,
More than all blood of bulls and goats, the will
That, self-forgetting, lives in deeds like this."
So spake the hero-king, and all the host
Looked on and wondered ; and those noble three,
The mightiest of the thirty, felt their souls
Knit closer to King David and to God.

E. H. PLUMPTRE

35

THE RAISING OF SAMUEL

Thou whose spell can raise the dead,
Bid the prophet's form appear.
"Samuel, raise thy buried head!
King, behold the phantom seer!"

THE RAISING OF SAMUEL.

Earth yawn'd ; he stood the centre of a cloud :
Light changed its hue, retiring from his shroud.
Death stood all glassy in his fixed eye ;
His hand was wither'd, and his veins were dry ;
His foot, in bony whiteness, glitter'd there,
Shrunken and sinewless, and ghastly bare :
From lips that moved not and unbreathing frame,
Like cavern'd winds, the hollow accents came.
Saul saw, and fell to earth, as falls the oak,
At once, and blasted by the thunder-stroke.

"Why is my sleep disquieted?
Who is he that calls the dead?
Is it thou, oh King? Behold,
Bloodless are these limbs, and cold :
Such are mine ; and such shall be
Thine to-morrow, when with me :
Ere the coming day is done,
Such shalt thou be, such thy son.
Fare thee well, but for a day,
Then we mix our mouldering clay.
Thou, thy race, lie pale and low,
Pierced by shafts of many a bow ;
And the falchion by thy side
To thy heart thy hand shall guide :
Crownless, breathless, headless fall,
Son and sire, the house of Saul!"

LORD BYRON

36
SONG OF SAUL BEFORE HIS LAST BATTLE

Warriors and chiefs! should the shaft or the sword
Pierce me in leading the host of the Lord,
Heed not the corse, though a king's in your path:
Bury your steel in the bosoms of Gath!

Thou who art bearing my buckler and bow,
Should the soldiers of Saul look away from the foe,
Stretch me that moment in blood at thy feet!
Mine be the doom which they dared not to meet.

Farewell to others, but never we part,
Heir to my royalty, son of my heart!
Bright is the diadem, boundless.the sway,
Or kingly the death, which awaits us to-day.

LORD BYRON

37
DAVID'S LAMENT OVER SAUL AND JONATHAN

2 Samuel i. 19-27.

Thy glory, O Israel, is slain upon thy high places!
How are the mighty fallen!
Tell it not in Gath,
Publish it not in the streets of Ashkelon;

Lest the daughters of the Philistines rejoice,
Lest the daughters of the uncircumcised triumph.
Ye mountains of Gilboa,
Let there be no dew nor rain upon you,
    neither fields of offerings:
For there the shield of the mighty was vilely cast
    away,
The shield of Saul, not anointed with oil.
From the blood of the slain, from the fat of the
    mighty,
The bow of Jonathan turned not back,
And the sword of Saul returned not empty.
Saul and Jonathan were lovely and pleasant in their
    lives,
And in their death they were not divided;
They were swifter than eagles,
They were stronger than lions.
Ye daughters of Israel, weep over Saul,
Who clothed you in scarlet delicately,
Who put ornaments of gold upon your apparel.
How are the mighty fallen in the midst of the
    battle!
Jonathan is slain upon thy high places.
I am distressed for thee, my brother Jonathan:
Very pleasant hast thou been unto me:
Thy love to me was wonderful,
Passing the love of women.
How are the mighty fallen,
And the weapons of war perished!

                BIBLE—REVISED VERSION

38

THE SONGS OF THE NIGHT

As David in his youthful days was tending his flocks on Bethlehem's plains, the spirit of the Lord came upon him, and his senses were opened that he might comprehend the songs of the night.

The heavens proclaimed the glory of God; the glittering stars all formed one chorus. Their harmonious melody resounded on earth, and the sweet fulness of their voices vibrated to its uttermost bounds.

"Light is the countenance of the Eternal," sung the setting sun. "I am the hem of his garment," responded the rosy tint of twilight.

The clouds gathered and said, "We are his nocturnal tent," and the waters of the cloud, and the hollow voices of the thunders, joined in the lofty chorus. "The voice of the Eternal is upon the waters; the God of glory thundereth; the Lord upon many waters."

"He did fly upon my wings," whispered the wind, and the silent air replied, "I am the breath of God, the aspiration of his benign presence."

"We hear the songs of praise," said the parched earth; "all around is praise, I alone am silent and mute!" And the falling dew replied, "I will nourish thee, so that thou shalt be refreshed and rejoice, and thy infants shall bloom like the young rose."

"Joyfully we bloom," replied the refreshed meadows. The full ears of corn waved as they sung, "We are the blessing of God, the hosts of God against famine."

"We bless you from above," said the moon; "We bless you," responded the stars; and the grasshopper chirped, "Me too He blesses in the pearly dew-drop."

"He quenched my thirst," said the roe; "and refreshed me," continued the stag; "and grants us our food," said the beasts of the forest, "and clothes my lambs," gratefully sung the sheep.

"He heard me," croaked the raven, "when I was forsaken and alone." "He heard me," said the wild goat of the rocks, "when my time came and I calved."

And the turtle-dove cooed, and the swallow and all the birds joined their song: "We have found our nests, our houses, we dwell on the altar of the Lord, and sleep under the shadow of his wing, in tranquillity and peace."

"And peace," replied the night, and echo prolonged the sound, when chanticleer awoke the dawn and crowed, "Open the portals, the gates of the world! The King of glory approacheth! Awake! Arise! Ye sons of men, give praises and thanks to the Lord, for the King of glory cometh."

. . . .

The sun arose and David awoke from his melodious rapture. But as long as he lived, the strains of creation's harmony remained in his soul, and daily he recalled them from the strings of his harp.

THE HEBREW REVIEW
Talmudic Allegory

39
THE DEDICATION OF THE TEMPLE

1 Kings viii. 22-62.

And Solomon placed himself before the altar of the Lord in the presence of all the congregation of Israel, and spread forth his hands toward heaven;

And he said, O Lord, the God of Israel, there is no God like thee, in the heavens above, and on the earth beneath, thou who keepest the covenant and the kindness for thy servants that walk before thee with all their heart;

Who hast kept for thy servant David my father what thou hadst promised him; and thou spokest with thy mouth, and hast fulfilled it with thy hand, as it is this day.

And now, O Lord, the God of Israel, keep for thy servant David my father what thou hast spoken concerning him, saying, There shall never fail thee a man in my sight who sitteth on the throne of Israel; if thy children but take heed to their way, to walk before me as thou hast walked before me.

And now, O God of Israel, I pray thee, let thy word be verified, which thou hast spoken unto thy servant David my father.

For in truth will God then dwell on the earth: behold, the heavens and the heavens of heavens cannot contain thee: how much less then this house that I have built!

Yet wilt thou turn thy regard unto the prayer of thy servant, and to his supplication, O Lord my

God, to listen unto the entreaty and unto the prayer, which thy servant prayeth before thee to-day;

That thy eyes may be open toward this house, night and day, toward the place of which thou hast said, My name shall be there, that thou mayest listen unto the prayer which thy servant shall pray at this place.

And listen thou to the supplication of thy servant and of thy people Israel, which they will pray at this place; and oh, do thou hear in heaven thy dwelling-place; and hear, and forgive.

If any man trespass against his neighbor, and an oath be laid upon him to cause him to swear, and the oath come before thy altar in this house:

Then do thou hear in heaven, and act, and judge thy servants, by condemning the wicked, to bring his way upon his head; and by justifying the righteous, to give him according to his righteousness.

When thy people Israel are struck down before the enemy, because they have sinned against thee, and they return then to thee, and confess thy name, and pray, and make supplication unto thee in this house:

Then do thou hear in heaven, and forgive the sin of thy people Israel, and cause them to return unto the land which thou hast given unto their fathers.

When the heavens be shut up, and there be no rain, because they have sinned against thee; and they pray toward this place, and confess thy name, and turn from their sin, because thou hast afflicted them:

Then do thou hear in heaven, and forgive the sin

of thy servants, and of thy people Israel; for thou wilt teach them the good way wherein they should walk; and give then rain upon thy land, which thou hast given to thy people for an inheritance.

If there be famine in the land, if there be pestilence, blasting, mildew, or if there be locust, caterpillar; if their enemy besiege them in the land in their gates; at whatsoever plague, whatsoever sickness:

What prayer and supplication soever be made by any man, of all thy people Israel, when they shall be conscious every man of the plague of his own heart, and he then spread forth his hands toward this house:

Then do thou hear in heaven the place of thy dwelling and forgive, and act, and give to every man in accordance with all his ways, as thou mayest know his heart; for thou, thyself alone, knowest the heart of all the children of men;

In order that they may fear thee all the days that they live on the face of the land which thou hast given to our fathers.

But also to the stranger, who is not of thy people Israel, but cometh out of a far-off country for the sake of thy name;

For they will hear of thy great name, and of thy strong hand, and of thy outstretched arm; when he will come and pray at this house:

Mayest thou listen in heaven, the place of thy dwelling, and do according to all that the stranger will call on thee for; in order that all the nations of the earth may know thy name, to fear thee, as do thy people Israel ; and that they may understand that this house, which I have built, is called by thy name.

If thy people go out to battle against their enemy, on the way on which thou mayest send them, and they do pray unto the Lord in the direction of the city which thou hast chosen and of the house that I have built for thy name:

Then hear thou in heaven their prayer and their supplication, and procure them justice.

If they sin against thee, (for there is no man that may not sin) and thou be angry with them, and give them up before the enemy, so that their captors carry them away captive unto the land of the enemy, be it far or near ;

And if they then take it to their heart in the land whither they have been carried captive, and repent, and make supplication unto thee in the land of their captors, saying, We have sinned, and have committed iniquity, we have acted wickedly ;

And they return unto thee with all their heart, and with all their soul, in the land of their enemies, who have led them away captive, and they pray unto thee in the direction of their land, which thou hast given unto their fathers, of the city which thou hast chosen, and of the house which I have built for thy name :

Then hear thou in heaven the place of thy dwelling their prayer and their supplication, and procure them justice.

And forgive thy people for what they have sinned against thee, and all their transgressions whereby they have transgressed against thee, and cause them to find mercy before their captors, that they may have mercy on them;

For they are thy people, and thy heritage, whom thou hast brought forth out of Egypt, from the midst of the iron furnace;

That thy eyes may be open unto the supplication of thy servant, and unto the supplication of thy people Israel, to listen unto them in all for which they call unto thee;

For thou hast separated them unto thee as a heritage from all the people of the earth, as thou spokest by the hand of Moses thy servant, when thou broughtest forth our fathers out of Egypt, O Lord Eternal.

And it happened, that, when Solomon had made an end of praying all this prayer and supplication unto the Lord, he arose from before the altar of the Lord from kneeling on his knees, with his hands spread out toward heaven.

And he stood up and blessed all the congregation of Israel, with a loud voice, saying,

Blessed be the Lord, who hath given rest unto his people Israel, in accordance with all that he hath spoken : so that there hath not failed one word of all his good promise, which he spoke by the hand of Moses his servant.

The Lord our God be with us, as he was with our fathers; oh may he not leave us, nor forsake us;

That he may incline our heart unto him, to walk in all his ways, and to keep his commandments, and his statutes, and his ordinances, which he commanded our fathers.

And may these my words, wherewith I have made supplication before the Lord, be nigh unto the Lord our God day and night, that he may maintain the cause of his servant, and the cause of his people Israel in their daily requirements.

In order that all the nations of the earth may know that the Lord is the true God, and none else.

Let your heart therefore be entire with the Lord your God, to walk in his statutes, and to keep his commandments, as at this day.

BIBLE—LEESER'S TRANSLATION

40

AZRAEL

(From *Tales of a Wayside Inn*)

King Solomon, before his palace gate
At evening, on the pavement tessellate
Was walking with a stranger from the East,
Arrayed in rich attire as for a feast,
The mighty Runjeet-Sing, a learned man,
And Rajah of the realms of Hindostan.
And as they walked the guest became aware
Of a white figure in the twilight air,
Gazing intent, as one who with surprise
His form and features seemed to recognize;
And in a whisper to the king he said:
"What is yon shape, that, pallid as the dead,
Is watching me, as if he sought to trace
In the dim light the features of my face?"

The king looked, and replied: "I know him well;
It is the Angel men call Azrael,
'Tis the Death Angel; what hast thou to fear?"
And the guest answered: "Lest he should come near,
And speak to me, and take away my breath!
Save me from Azrael, save me from death!
O king, that hast dominion o'er the wind,
Bid it arise and bear me hence to Ind."

The king gazed upward at the cloudless sky,
Whispered a word, and raised his hand on high,
And lo! the signet-ring of chrysoprase
On his uplifted finger seemed to blaze
With hidden fire, and rushing from the west
There came a mighty wind, and seized the guest
And lifted him from earth, and on they passed,
His shining garments streaming in the blast,
A silken banner o'er the walls upreared,
A purple cloud, that gleamed and disappeared.
Then said the Angel, smiling: "If this man
Be Rajah Runjeet-Sing of Hindostan,
Thou hast done well in listening to his prayer;
I was upon my way to seek him there."

H. W. LONGFELLOW

41

THE POOLS OF SOLOMON

(From *Tancred*)

I made great works: I built myself houses; I planted myself vineyards:

I made myself gardens and orchards, and planted therein trees of all kinds of fruit;

I made myself pools of water, to water therewith the forest overgrown with trees.—ECCLESIASTES ii. 4-6.

About an hour after leaving Bethlehem, in a secluded valley, is one of the few remaining public works of the great Hebrew kings. It is in every respect worthy of them. I speak of those colossal reservoirs cut out of the native rock and fed by a single spring, discharging their waters into an aqueduct of perforated stone, which, until a comparatively very recent period, still conveyed them to Jerusalem. They are three in number, of varying lengths from five to six hundred feet, and almost as broad; their depth still undiscovered. They communicate with each other, so that the water of the uppermost reservoir, flowing through the intermediate one, reached the third, which fed the aqueduct. They are lined with a hard cement like that which coats the pyramids, and which remains uninjured; and it appears that hanging gardens once surrounded them. The Arabs still call these reservoirs the pools of Solomon, nor is there any reason to doubt the tradition. Tradition, perhaps often more faithful than written documents, is a sure and almost infallible guide in the minds of the people where there has been no complicated variety of historic incidents to confuse and break the chain of memory; where their rare revolutions have consisted of an eruption once in a thousand years into the cultivated world; where society has never been broken up, but their domestic manners have remained the same; where, too, they revere truth, and are rigid in its oral delivery, since that is their only means of disseminating knowledge.

There is no reason to doubt that these reservoirs were the works of Solomon. This secluded valley, then, was once the scene of his imaginative and delicious life. Here were his pleasure gardens; these slopes were covered with his fantastic terraces, and the high places glittered with his pavilions. The fountain that supplied these treasured waters was perhaps the "sealed fountain," to which he compared his bride; and here was the garden palace where the charming Queen of Sheba vainly expected to pose the wisdom of Israel, as she held at a distance before the most dexterous of men the two garlands of flowers, alike in form and color, and asked the great king, before his trembling court, to decide which of the wreaths was the real one.

They are gone, they are vanished—these deeds of beauty and these words of wit! The bright and glorious gardens of the tiaraed poet and the royal sage, that once echoed with his lyric voice, or with the startling truths of his pregnant aphorisms, end in this wild and solitary valley.

. . . .

Why—what—is this desolation? Why are there no more kings, whose words are the treasured wisdom of countless ages and the mention of whose name to this moment thrills the heart of the Oriental, from the waves of the midland ocean to the broad rivers of the farthest Ind? Why are there no longer bright-witted queens to step out of their Arabian palaces and pay visits to the gorgeous "house of the forest of Lebanon," or to where Baalbec, or Tadmor in the wilderness, rose on those plains now strewn with the superb relics of their inimitable magnificence?

And yet some flat-nosed Frank, full of bustle and puffed up with self-conceit, a race spawned perhaps in the morasses of some northern forest hardly yet cleared,—talks of Progress! Progress to what, and from whence? Amid empires shrivelled into deserts, amid the wrecks of great cities, a single column or obelisk of which nations import for the prime ornament of their mud-built capitals, amid arts forgotten, commerce annihilated, fragmentary literatures and populations destroyed, the European talks of progress, because, by an ingenious application of some scientific acquirements, he has established a society which has mistaken comfort for civilization.

BENJAMIN DISRAELI

42

THE QUEEN OF THE SOUTH

(Extract)

Our ships went forth from Sheba's ports,
  They sailed up Edom's sea,
We passed the shores where Joktan's sons
  Roam wild, and fierce, and free;
Where Elath's harbor opens wide,
  And then, in stately march,
Where Bozrah's rocks are crowned with towers,
  And spanned by loftiest arch.

We looked upon the accursèd sea,
  We breathed its sulphurous breath,
Where bleaching bones, and scurf of salt,
  Speak evermore of death;
We crossed, where stately Jordan flows
  By many a grove of palm,
Where fragrant winds from Gilead bring
  Their gentle airs of balm.

Then up the vale whose rocks o'erhang
  The path of winter stream,
Until at last on wistful eyes
  The towers of Zion gleam;
Where olives gray and hoar grow thick,
  We saw the vision bright;
The golden city, Home of Peace,
  Burst full upon our sight.

We saw the thousand bright-eyed youths
  In purple stiff with gold;
We saw the hosts of Israel march,
  Ten thousand warriors bold;
The chariot such as Pharaoh owns,
The banners waving wide,
The throne where six proud lions stand
  As guards on either side.

But most where slopes the wide ascent
  To where Jehovah dwells,
Where still from choir of white-robed priests
  The Hallelujah swells;
Where, clad in purple robes from Tyre,
  He enters from the East,
The king, who walks in glorious state,
  Half-monarch, and half-priest.

We met; his eye glowed bright and free,
  I heard his speech distil,
Like wild bees' store of crystal gold,
  And heart and spirit fill;
He did not scorn my woman's thoughts,
  My passion's eager quest;
His noblest words, his treasured lore,
  My spirit's cravings blest.

I asked, "O king, the nations bow
  To Gods on many a throne,
And many a name with song and dance
  As King and Lord they own;

But which of all shall we adore
  As giving life and light,
What name may best His favor win,
  The Lord of boundless might?"

He answered, "Lo! the Lord is One,
  Above the heaven He dwells,
And day to night His power declares,
  And night to morning tells;
Give Him thy heart: in truth and love
  Do thou His righteous will,
And He, thy Father, Lord of all,
  Shall all thy wish fulfil!"

I asked, "O king, the skies are drear,
  We wage a fruitless strife;
The heart is faint, the hands hang down,
  We weary of our life;
We toil in vain for wealth and fame,
  We gather and we waste;
Yet fail to find the bread of life,
  The food the angels taste."

And he, "Who walks in light and truth,
  Shall find the fount of joy,
The peace which naught on earth can give,
  No power of man destroy;
The child-like heart, the fear of God,
  Is truest wisdom found;
And joy and goodness circle still
  In one unbroken round."

I asked, "O king! the ways of God,
   They baffle and perplex;
The evil prosper, nothing comes
   Their full-fed souls to vex;
The righteous perish, crushed and scorned;
   Their life in darkness ends;
Is this the order and the truth
   Unerring counsel sends?"

He answered, "Lo, thou see'st as yet
   The outskirts of His rule;
He trains the child, He forms the man
   In suffering's varied school;
Dire forms of evil hover still
   Around the proud's success,
And thoughts of trust, and hope, and peace
   The righteous mourner bless."

I asked, "Yet once again, O king,
   This life, can it be all?
We toil and strive our little day,
   And then the shadows fall;
Have we no goal to reach at last?
   Has this wild sea no shore?
Has God no home where wearied souls
   May rest for evermore?"

And he, "The things behind the veil
   No mortal yet hath known;
On that far land the shadows rest
   That shroud the Eternal Throne;

Yet this we know, in life or death,
    His presence still is there;
And where that brightness fills the soul,
    Is joy beyond compare."

So communed I, and every word
    Went straight to heart and soul,
Dim thoughts made clear, and random will
    Now striving for the goal;
I drank deep draughts of that clear fount,
    The well of life and truth,
As one new-born I went my way
    In gladness, as of youth.

And now the past is past; again
    On Sheba's coasts I dwell,
And never more my feet shall tread
    Where Jordan's flood-streams swell;
Yet still the days that then I knew
    Are worth long years to me,
And in the visions of the night
    That princely form I see.

                    E. H. PLUMPTRE

43

THE YOUTHFUL SOLOMON

When the Lord first appeared to the youthful Solomon, in a vision of the night, He said unto him, "Ask what I shall give thee."

And behold the youth prayed not for silver or

gold, for honor, fame, or long life. His prayer was, "Grant me wisdom;" and with her, the daughter of the Most High, he received every felicity for which he could have prayed.

To her he dedicated his most beautiful songs. Her he recommended to the sons of men as the only true source of happiness. As long as he continued faithful to her, he rejoiced in the blessing of God, in the love and admiration of men. And it is only through her that his fame survives, and has been preserved from oblivion.

THE AGED SOLOMON

Luxury, riches, and ambition perverted the ripened manhood of Solomon; he forgot wisdom, the pride of his youth, and his heart became lost in the vortex of frivolous dissipation and wicked folly.

Once as he was walking in his splendid gardens, he heard the conversation of the manifold creatures around him; for he understood the language of beast and of bird, of tree, stone, and shrub; he turned his ear, and he listened.

"Behold," said the lily, "there goes the king; he passes me in his pride, whilst I, in my humility, am robed more splendidly than he."

And the palm tree waved its boughs, and said, "There he goes; the oppressor of his country; and yet his vile flatterers, in their fulsome songs, presume to compare him to me. But where are his boughs? where the fruit with which he gladdens the hearts of men?"

He went on, and heard the nightingale sing to her beloved: "As we love each other, Solomon loveth not—O, not one of his sultanas holds him dear as I do thee, my dearest!"

And the turtle-dove cooed to her mate, "Not one of his thousand wives would grieve for his loss, as I would for thine, my only beloved."

The enraged monarch hastened his pace, and he came to the nest, where the stork was teaching her young to launch forth on the adventurous flight.

"What I do for you," said the stork to its brood, "King Solomon does not do for his son Rehoboam. He does not teach and exhort him; therefore the young prince will not thrive. Strangers will lord it over his father's domains."

The king withdrew to his secret closet; musing, he sat there in silent grief.

As he sat there, sunk in painful reflections, the bride of his youthful years, Wisdom, stood invisible before him, and touched his eyelids. He fell into a deep sleep, and had a mournful vision. He saw the deputation of the tribes as they stood before his haughty son. He saw his empire divided through the silly answer of the foolish boy. He saw ten of the tribes he had oppressed rebel, and place a stranger on their throne. He saw his palaces in ruins; his garden rooted up; the city destroyed; the temple of the Lord in ashes. Suddenly he awoke from his sleep, and terror seized on his tremulous mind.

When lo! once more the bride of his youth, the guardian of his early career, stood visible before him. Tears flowed from her eyes. She spoke: "Thou hast seen what hereafter will happen. Thou alone art the first cause of all these calamities. But it is not in thy power to recall or to alter the past; for thou canst not bid the river to flow back to its springs, nor the years of thy youth to return. Thy soul is wearied, thy heart is exhausted, and I, the forsaken of thy youth, can no more be thy companion in the land of terrestrial life."

With pity in her looks, she vanished; and Solomon, who had crowned his youthful days with roses, wrote in his old age a book on the vanity of all human affairs on earth.

THE HEBREW REVIEW
Talmudic Allegories

44

ELIJAH'S INTERVIEW

1 Kings xix. 11-13.

On Horeb's rock the prophet stood,—
  The Lord before him passed;
A hurricane in angry mood
  Swept by him strong and fast;
The forest fell before its force,
The rocks were shivered in its course,
  God was not in the blast;
'Twas but the whirlwind of his breath,
Announcing danger, wreck, and death.

It ceased. The air grew mute,—a cloud
  Came muffling up the sun;
When through the mountain, deep and loud,
  An earthquake thundered on;
The frighted eagle sprang in air,
The wolf ran howling from his lair,—
  God was not in the storm;—
'Twas but the rolling of his car,—
The trampling of his steeds from far.

'Twas still again,—and Nature stood
  And calmed her ruffled frame;
When swift from heaven a fiery flood
  To earth devouring came;
Down to the depth the ocean fled,—
The sick'ning sun looked wan and dead,
  Yet God filled not the flame;—
'Twas but the terror of his eye,
That lightened through the troubled sky.

At last a voice, all still and small,
  Rose sweetly on the ear;
Yet rose so shrill and clear, that all
  In heaven and earth might hear.
It spoke of peace, it spoke of love,
It spoke as angels speak above,
  And God himself was there!
For O, it was a Father's voice
That bade the trembling heart rejoice!

CAMPBELL

45

ELIJAH

Elijah was of a fiery spirit; and with a spirit of fire he performed his prophetic office. He called flames down from heaven, and consumed his own life in his zeal.

Weary and exhausted, he withdrew from the haunts of men; in the dreary desert he threw himself under a juniper tree, and sighed, "It is enough! Now, O Lord, take my soul unto thee."

And an angel of the Lord strengthened him; and he reached the mountain of Horeb, where the Lord removed the burden of his prophetic calling off his shoulders, and directed him to anoint another in his stead.

And when, with the anointed Elisha, Elijah came to the river Jordan, a fiery chariot and fiery horses appeared; the two companions were separated, and Elijah ascended to the throne.

The first who appeared to him in the regions of bliss was Moses, his prototype. He reached Elijah his right hand, through the purifying flames of the fiery chariot, and said to him, "Thou hast been zealous, my brother, thy zeal has been ardent, and thou hast suffered much from thy brethren, I too have suffered the like; still I prayed for their preservation, and offered my soul as a ransom for theirs. Nevertheless, approach the throne of the

Judge, the All-merciful." With trembling steps Elijah advanced to the cloud of the throne.

"What doest thou here, Elijah?" demanded a voice from out of the throne. He answered, "I have been very zealous for the Lord God of Hosts; for Israel have forsaken thy covenant, thrown down thy altars, and slain thy prophets with the sword; I, only I, was left, and they sought my life to take it away."

And a fire went forth from the clouds; but the Lord was not in the fire. And a wind went forth from the cloud; strong and irresistible, it rent the mountains, and brake in pieces the rocks; but the Lord was not in the wind.

The wind and the fire had passed, when a still small voice was heard. A sensation never before experienced penetrated the prophet, and the flame of his spirit became chastened like the radiance of dawn.

"Rest thou here," said the voice, "repose and gain new vigor after thy toils; for the Lord is merciful and benevolent. Thou shalt often again descend to the sons of men; thou shalt teach, but with mild kindness; thou shalt console and aid them with thy love, nor longer punish them in thy zeal: for the Lord is gracious."

And often since then has Elijah visited mankind, but in a different spirit from that which animated him during his earthly sojourn. What before was ardent jealousy, is now loving kindness; what was fiery zeal is now mildness and benevolence. Invisible, or in an assumed shape, he guides the conversation of those who seek true wisdom, and unites their souls. He it is who turns the hearts of the fathers to their children, and the hearts of the children to their parents. Harbinger of good, he aids the righteous in the hour of danger, and is ever present to solace and strengthen those who pray.

His office is to proclaim to mankind the coming of the great and dreadful day of the Lord.

THE HEBREW REVIEW
Talmudic Allegory

46
OH! WEEP FOR THOSE

Oh! weep for those that wept by Babel's stream,
Whose shrines are desolate, whose land a dream;
Weep for the harp of Judah's broken shell;
Mourn—where their God has dwelt the Godless dwell!

And where shall Israel lave her bleeding feet?
And where shall Zion's songs again seem sweet?
And Judah's melody once more rejoice
The hearts that leap'd before its heavenly voice?

Tribes of the wandering foot and weary breast,
How shall ye flee away and be at rest!
The wild-dove hath her nest, the fox his cave,
Mankind their country—Israel but the grave.

LORD BYRON

47

THE JEWISH CAPTIVE

Lo! where Euphrates, in his tranquil bed,
    Scarce swells his heaving bosom to the light,
While from the west a thousand hues are shed,
    To deck his waters, ere the sombre night
Shall on his gorgeous palaces come down,
And shroud each glory in his darkened frown.

    .   .   .   .

Forth from a marble fount the waters splash,
    And twinkle down in many a mimic fall—
That ever in the light like diamonds flash;
    And in their melody they seem to call
To old Euphrates, as he wanders by,
And spreads his waters to the golden sky.

A group of maidens by the willows bend,
    And weave their tresses by the twilight sky,
While ever on the air glad voices blend,
    And many a song and laugh are floating by
To mingle with the sound of chiming waters,
That lave the feet of dark-eyed Syrian daughters.

"Lo! here," cries one, "the captive Mara tends,—
    Mara, the Jewess, queenlike in her woe;
Though many a victor to her beauty bends,
    The smile no more her gentle lips may know.
Not for her own she weeps, but Judah's wrongs,
And pours her sorrows in their mystic songs.

"Didst ever hear the music strange and high,
  The Jewish captives from their harp-strings
    bring,
While Zion-ward they turn the kindling eye?
  Mara, approach; we fain would hear thee sing
A song of Zion—such as once ye sang
When Jordan's waters to the music rang."

The captive flung her tresses from her brow,
  And upward raised her dark and tearless eye—
Clasped her pale hands in agony of woe,
  And heaved her breast with many a smothered
    sigh;
Quick thronging visions o'er her spirit passed—
She lived again where childhood's lot was cast.

Lo! sad Judea's vine-clad hills are there
  And fruitful Jordan, with its many streams,—
Proud Lebanon, with cedars tall and fair,—
  And, midst her desolation, sadly gleams
Lone Zion, widowed, childless, and oppressed,
A Rachel for her first-born son distressed.

There, 'neath a cottage, where the trailing vine
  In many a festoon o'er the lattice clings,
An ancient matron seems alone to pine,
  And calls her children, while her arms she flings,
To clasp the shadows that her fancies raise,
The cherished offspring of her happier days.

But what is grief like hers—that matron old,
  Who spreads her white locks to the evening sky,

When Zion stands bereft—her altars cold !
And all her exiled children turn their eye
To where the happier swallow builds her nest,
And in the courts of God has found her rest.

O'er Mara's soul the power of music rushed,—
　Her harp the maidens from the willows bring :
Forth from her lips high thoughts and feelings
　　gushed,
" How can I Zion's songs, a captive, sing ?
How sing of Jordan, here by Babel's strand ?
How sing of Judah, in this dark, strange land ?

　　　Oh Zion ! if I cease for thee
　　　　My earliest vows to pay—
　　　If for thy sad and ruined walls
　　　　I ever cease to pray—
　　　If I no more thy sacred courts
　　　　With holy reverence prize,
　　　Or Zion-ward shall cease to turn
　　　　My ever-longing eyes—
　　　Or if the splendor round me thrown
　　　　Shall touch this Jewish heart,
　　　And make me cease to prize thy joy
　　　　Above all other art,—
　　　Oh ! may this hand no more with skill
　　　　E'er touch this sacred string,
　　　And may this tongue grow cold in death,
　　　　Ere I shall cease to sing
　　　And pray for Zion's holy courts,
　　　　Or dare to bow the knee
　　　To these poor, blind and helpless gods,
　　　　Forgetful, Lord, of thee."

　　　　　　　　　ELIZABETH OAKES SMITH

48

IDOLATRY

Isaiah xliv. 12-20.

The iron-smith maketh an axe and worketh it in the coals, and with hammers he fashioneth it and worketh it with his powerful arm; he also, when he is hungry, loseth his strength; when he drinketh no water, he becometh faint.

The worker in wood stretcheth out the rule; he marketh it out with chalk; he fitteth it with planes, —and he marketh it out with the compass, and maketh it after the figure of a man, after the beauty of a child of earth, that it may dwell in a house.

He felleth for himself cedars, and taketh cypress and oak, and he chooseth for himself the strongest among the trees of the forest; he planteth an ash, and the rain causeth it to grow.

Then doth it serve a man for burning; and he taketh thereof, and warmeth himself; he also heateth therewith, and baketh bread; he also worketh out a god, and boweth himself; he maketh of it an image, and kneeleth down thereto.

The half thereof hath he burnt in fire; with the half thereof will he eat flesh; he will roast food, and be satisfied; he will also warm himself, and say, Aha! I am warm, I have felt the fire:

And the residue thereof hath he made into a god, his graven image; he kneeleth down unto it, and boweth himself, and prayeth unto it; and saith, Deliver me; for my god art thou.

They know not, they understand not; for their
eyes are daubed over, that they cannot see; their
hearts, that they cannot understand.

And he layeth it not to heart, and hath no knowl-
edge, no understanding to say, The half thereof
have I burnt in fire; and I have also baked upon
its coals bread; I now will roast flesh, and eat it;
and shall I make of its residue an abomination,
before a block of wood shall I kneel?

He pursueth ashes; a deceived heart hath turned
him aside; and he cannot deliver his soul, and will
not say, is there not a lie in my right hand?

BIBLE—LEESER'S TRANSLATION

49

THE FALSE GODS

(From *Paradise Lost*)

First Moloch, horrid king, besmeared with blood
Of human sacrifice, and parents' tears;
Though, for the noise of drums and timbrels loud,
Their children's cries unheard, that passed through
    fire
To his grim idol. Him the Ammonite
Worshipped in Rabba and her watery plain,
In Argob and in Basan, to the stream
Of utmost Arnon. Nor content with such
Audacious neighborhood, the wisest heart
Of Solomon he led by fraud to build
His temple right against the temple of God
On that opprobrious hill, and made his grove

The pleasant valley of Hinnom, Tophet thence
And black Gehenna called, the type of Hell.
Next Chemos, the obscene dread of Moab's sons,
From Aroar to Nebo and the wild
Of southmost Abarim ; in Hesebon
And Horonaim, Seon's realm, beyond
The flowery dale of Sibma clad with vines,
And Elealé to the Asphaltic Pool :
Peor his other name, when he enticed
Israel in Sittim, on their march from Nile,'
To do him wanton rites, which cost them woe.
Yet thence his lustful orgies he enlarged
Even to that hill of scandal, by the grove
Of Moloch homicide, lust hard by hate,
Till good Josiah drove them thence to Hell.
With these came they who, from the bordering
 flood

Of old Euphrates to the brook that parts
Egypt from Syrian ground, had general names
Of Baalim and Ashtaroth—those male,
These feminine. For spirits, when they please,
Can either sex assume, or both ; so soft
And uncompounded is their essence pure,
Not tied or manacled with joint or limb,
Nor founded on the brittle strength of bones,
Like cumbrous flesh ; but, in what shape they
 choose,

Dilated or condensed, bright or obscure,
Can execute their aery purposes,
And works of love or enmity fulfil.

For those the race of Israel oft forsook
Their Living Strength, and unfrequented left
His righteous altar, bowing lowly down
To bestial gods; for which their heads, as low
Bowed down in battle, sunk before the spear
Of despicable foes. With these in troop
Came Astoreth, whom the Phœnicians called
Astarte, queen of heaven, with crescent horns;
To whose bright image nightly by the moon
Sidonian virgins paid their vows and songs;
In Sion also not unsung, where stood
Her temple on the offensive mountain, built
By that uxorious king whose heart, though large,
Beguiled by fair idolatresses, fell
To idols foul. Thammuz came next behind,
Whose annual wound in Lebanon allured
The Syrian damsels to lament his fate
In amorous ditties all a summer's day,
While smooth Adonis from his native rock
Ran purple to the sea, supposed with blood
Of Thammuz yearly wounded: the love-tale
Infected Sion's daughters with like heat,
Whose wanton passions in the sacred porch
Ezekiel saw, when, by the vision led,
His eye surveyed the dark idolatries
Of alienated Judah. Next came one
Who mourned in earnest, when the captive ark
Maimed his brute image, head and hands lopt off
In his own temple, on the grunsel-edge,
Where he fell flat, and shamed his worshippers:
Dagon his name, sea-monster, upward man
And downward fish; yet had his temple high

Reared in Azotus, dreaded through the coast
Of Palestine, in Gath, and Ascalon,
And Accaron, and Gaza's frontier bounds.
Him followed Rimmon, whose delightful seat
Was fair Damascus, on the fertile banks
Of Abbana and Pharphar, lucid streams.
He also against the house of God was bold:
A leper once he lost, and gained a king—
Ahaz, his sottish conqueror, whom he drew
God's altar to disparage, and displace
For one of Syrian mode, whereon to burn
His odious offerings, and adore the gods
Whom he had vanquished. After these appeared
A crew who, under names of old renown—
Osiris, Isis, Orus, and their train—
With monstrous shapes and sorceries abused
Fanatic Egypt and her priests to seek
Their wandering gods disguised in brutish forms
Rather than human. Nor did Israel scape
The infection, when their borrowed gold composed
The calf in Oreb; and the rebel king
Doubled that sin in Bethel and in Dan,
Likening his Maker to the grazèd ox—
Jehovah, who, in one night, when he passed
From Egypt marching, equalled with one stroke
Both her first-born, and all her bleating gods.

JOHN MILTON

50

THE CAPTIVITY

(From *Bible Characters*)

Humanly speaking, what chance was there that Israelites or Jews would unlearn idolatry at Babylon? Why, what had all their idolatry come of? Imitation. Under the early Judges they could not, as a nation, withstand the example of a few conquered idolaters who worshipped false gods in groves for want of temples. In the height of their glory their wisest king was decoyed into idolatry by the example of his intellectual inferiors, his wives and concubines. Imitation and example set them bowing at one time to a contemptible fish-god; at another to a fiend whose worship entailed the burning of their children. Now, at Babylon idolatry was example and authority into the bargain. At Babylon idolatry was glorious, sublime; had every charm and seduction to win the sensual understanding and divert it from the unseen God.

If you and I and an archangel had been endowed with absolute power, but left to our own wisdom, human and angelic, I am persuaded that neither that archangel nor you nor I should have sent the Hebrews to Babylon to unlearn idolatry; so wide and impassable is the gulf between the sagacity of created beings and the genuine prescience that marks their Creator—for constant prescience implies omniscience. Babylon, bright centre of captivating idolatry, commenced an everlasting cure of Jewish idolatry, which punishments, blessings, miracles, could never effect in the land of Canaan. . . . .

Meantime, "sweet were the uses of adversity." The captivity roused great examples of faith, revived the necessity for miracles —and so miracles came—re-awakened the lyre of Judah, which had slept since the days of David, and stirred up the noblest army of prophets that ever preached in any period of Hebrew story.

. . . . Ere long that impregnable city, Babylon, falsified its past history, defied all human probability, and bowed to Hebrew prophecy. . .

Cyrus, descendant of the conqueror, had no sooner succeeded to the throne of Persia, to which Babylon and Palestine were now equally subject, than he issued a most remarkable edict ; he alleged Divine inspiration, and by order of the Most High —as he declared—invited the Jews to go up to Jerusalem and build the Temple to Him whom he, Cyrus, proclaimed to be the true God. He restored to the Jews their sacred vessels, and assisted them with his vast resources.

. . . . When the returned captives laid the foundation of the new Temple, there came a touch of nature which never, whilst books endure, shall pass from the memory of mankind. The young and the middle-aged praised God with shouts of joy; but many of the priests and Levites, who were ancient men, and had seen the first Temple in its glory, wept with a loud voice ; so that such as stood apart could not discern the noise of the shouts of joy from the noise of the wailing of those aged men.

Yet the leaders of the heathen nations that were settled in Judea baffled this good work by their intrigues for twenty-one years, and then at last the Temple was built and dedicated.

CHARLES READE

51
BY THE RIVERS OF BABYLON WE SAT DOWN AND WEPT

We sat down and wept by the waters
    Of Babel, and thought of the day
When our foe in the hue of his slaughters,
    Made Salem's high places his prey;
And ye, oh her desolate daughters!
    Were scatter'd all weeping away.

While sadly we gazed on the river
    Which roll'd on in freedom below,
They demanded the song; but, oh never
    That triumph the stranger shall know!
May this right hand be wither'd forever,
    Ere it string our high harp for the foe!

On the willow that harp is suspended,
    Oh Salem! its sound should be free;
And the hour when thy glories were ended
    But left me that token of thee:
And ne'er shall its soft tones be blended
    With the voice of the spoiler by me.

LORD BYRON

52

BUT WHO SHALL SEE

But who shall see the glorious day
  When, throned on Zion's brow,
The Lord shall rend that veil away
  Which hides the nations now?
When earth no more beneath the fear
  Of his rebuke shall lie;
When pain shall cease, and every tear
  Be wiped from every eye.

Then, Judah, thou no more shalt mourn
  Beneath the heathen's chain;
Thy days of splendor shall return,
  And all be new again.
The Fount of Life shall then be quaff'd
  In peace by all who come!
And every wind that blows shall waft
  Some long-lost exile home!

THOMAS MOORE

53

A PRAYER OF TOBIAS

Tobit xiii.

Bless'd be that King, Which evermore shall reign,
So ever may His Kingdom blessed be!
Which punisheth and pitieth again,
Which sends to hell and likewise setteth free;
  Before Whose Presence may no creature stand,
  Nor anything avoid His heavy Hand.

Ye children of His chosen Israel,
Before the Gentiles still confess His Name,
With whom He hath appointed you to dwell,
Even there, I say, extol and laud His fame :
    He is a Lord and God most gracious,
    And still hath been a Father unto us.

He will scourge us for our iniquity ;
Yet mercy will He take on us again,
And from those nations gatherèd shall we be,
With whom as strangers now we do remain,
    If in your hearts He shall repentance find,
    And turn to Him with zeal and willing mind.

When as your dealings shall be found upright,
Then will He turn His Face from you no more,
Nor thenceforth hide His Presence from your sight,
But lend His mercy then, laid up in store ;
    Therefore confess His Name, and praises sing
    To that most Great and Highest Heavenly King.

I will confess Him in captivity,
And to a wicked people show His might :
O turn to Him, vile sinners that you be,
And do the thing is upright in His sight !
    Who's there can tell if He will mercy show
    Or take compassion on you, yea or no ?

I will extol and laud Thy Name always,
My soul, the praise of Heaven's King express ;
All tongues on earth shall spread abroad His praise,
All nations show forth His righteousness ;
    Jerusalem, thou shalt be scourgèd then,
    But He will spare the sons of righteous men.

Fail not to give the Lord His praises due,
And still extol that Everlasting King;
And help to build His tabernacle new,
In which His saints shall ever sit and sing,
> In which the captives shall have end of grief,
> In which the poor shall ever find relief.

Many shall come from countries far and near,
And shall great gifts unto His Presence bring;
Many before His Presence shall appear
And shall rejoice in this Great Heavenly King:
> Cursèd be those which hate Thy Blessed Name,
> But bless'd be those which love and like the same.

Triumph with joy, ye that be good and just;
Though scatter'd now, yet shall ye gatherèd be;
Then in the Lord fix all your hope and trust,
And rest in peace till you these blessings see:
> Blessed be those which have been touch'd with grief,
> When they have seen thee scourg'd and want relief.

Those only shall rejoice with thee again,
And those shall be partakers of thy glory,
And shall in bliss for aye with thee remain,
Now passèd once these troubles transitory:
> Then, O my soul, see thou rejoice and sing,
> And laud the Great and Highest Heavenly King.

And He will build Jerusalem full fair
With emeralds and with sapphires of great price:
With precious stones He will her walls repair,
Her towers of gold with work of rare device;

And all her streets with beryl will He pave,
With carbuncles and ophirs passing brave:

And all her people there shall sit and say,
Praised be God with Alleluiah!

MICHAEL DRAYTON

54

VISION OF BELSHAZZAR

The King was on his throne,
  The Satraps throng'd the hall;
A thousand bright lamps shone
  O'er that high festival.
A thousand cups of gold,
  In Judah deemed divine—
Jehovah's vessels hold
  The godless Heathen's wine!

In that same hour and hall
  The fingers of a hand
Came forth against the wall,
  And wrote as if on sand:
The fingers of a man;—
  A solitary hand
Among the letters ran,
  And traced them like a wand.

The monarch saw, and shook,
  And bade no more rejoice;
All bloodless wax'd his look,
  And tremulous his voice.

"Let the men of lore appear,
　The wisest of the earth,
And expound the words of fear,
　Which mar our royal mirth."

Chaldea's seers are good,
　But here they have no skill;
And the unknown letters stood
　Untold and awful still.
And Babel's men of age
　Are wise and deep in lore;
But now they were not sage,
　They saw—but knew no more.

A captive in the land,
　A stranger and a youth,
He heard the king's command,
　He saw that writing's truth.
The lamps around were bright,
　The prophecy in view;
He read it on that night,—
　The morrow proved it true.

"Belshazzar's grave is made,
　His kingdom pass'd away,
He, in the balance weigh'd,
　Is light and worthless clay,
The shroud, his robe of state,
　His canopy the stone;
The Mede is at his gate!
　The Persian on his throne!"

LORD BYRON

55
BELSHAZZAR

Belshazzar is king! Belshazzar is lord!
And a thousand dark nobles all bend at his board;
Fruits glisten, flowers blossom, meats steam, and a
    flood
Of the wine that man loveth runs redder than blood;
Wild dancers are there, and a riot of mirth,
And the beauty that maddens the passions of
    earth;
And the crowds all shout, till the vast roofs ring—
All praise to Belshazzar, Belshazzar the king!"

"Bring forth," cries the monarch, "the vessels of
    gold,
Which my father tore down from the temples of old;
Bring forth, and we'll drink, while the trumpets
    are blown,
To the gods of bright silver, of gold, and of stone;
Bring forth!" and before him the vessels all shine,
And he bows unto Baal, and he drinks the dark
    wine,
While the trumpets bray, and the cymbals ring,—
"Praise, praise to Belshazzar, Belshazzar the king!"

Now what cometh—look, look!—without menace
    or call?
Who writes with the lightning's bright hand on
    the wall?

What pierceth the king like the point of a dart?
What drives the bold blood from his cheek to his
   heart?
"Chaldeans! Magicians! the letters expound!"
They are read,—and Belshazzar is dead on the
   ground!
Hark!—The Persian is come on a conqueror's wing;
And a Mede's on the throne of Belshazzar the king.

B. W. PROCTOR

56
EZEKIEL
Ezekiel xxxiii. 30-33.

They hear Thee not, O God! nor see;
Beneath Thy rod they mock at Thee;
The princes of our ancient line
Lie drunken with Assyrian wine;
The priests around Thy altar speak
The false words which their hearers seek;
And hymns which Chaldea's wanton maids
Have sung in Dura's idol-shades
Are with the Levites' chant ascending,
With Zion's holiest anthems blending!

On Israel's bleeding bosom set,
The heathen heel is crushing yet;
The towers upon our holy hill
Echo Chaldean footsteps still.
Our wasted shrines,—who weeps for them?
Who mourneth for Jerusalem?

Who turneth from his gains away?
Whose knee with mine is bowed to pray?
Who leaving feast and purpling cup,
Takes Zion's lamentation up?

A sad and thoughtful youth, I went
With Israel's early banishment;
And where the sullen Chebar crept,
The ritual of my fathers kept.
The water from the trench I drew,
The firstling of the flock I slew,
And, standing at the altar's side,
I shared the Levites' lingering pride,
That still amidst her mocking foes,
The smoke of Zion's offering rose.

In sudden whirlwind cloud and flame,
The Spirit of the Highest came!
Before mine eyes a vision passed,
A glory terrible and vast;
With dreadful eyes of living things,
And sounding sweep of angel-wings,
With circling light and sapphire throne,
And flame-like form of One thereon,
And voice of that dread Likeness sent
Down from the crystal firmament!

The burden of a prophet's power
Fell on me in that fearful hour;
From off unutterable woes
The curtain of the future rose;
I saw far down the coming time
The fiery chastisement of crime;

With noise of mingling hosts, and jar
Of falling towers and shouts of war,
I saw the nations rise and fall,
Like fire-gleams on my tent's white wall.

In dream and trance, I saw the slain
Of Egypt heaped like harvest grain.
I saw the walls of sea-born Tyre
Swept over by the spoiler's fire;
And heard the low, expiring moan
Of Edom on his rocky throne;
And, woe is me! the wild lament
From Zion's desolation sent;
And felt within my heart each blow
Which laid her holy places low.

In bonds and sorrow, day by day,
Before the pictured tile I lay;
And there, as in a mirror, saw
The coming of Assyria's war;
Her swarthy lines of spearmen pass
Like locusts through Bethhoron's grass;
I saw them draw their stormy hem
Of battle round Jerusalem;
And, listening, heard the Hebrew wail
Blend with the victor-trump of Baal!

Who trembled at my warning word?
Who owned the prophet of the Lord?
How mocked the rude, how scoffed the vile,
How stung the Levites' scornful smile,
As o'er my spirit, dark and slow,
The shadow crept of Israel's woe,

As if the angel's mournful roll
Had left its record on my soul,
And traced in lines of darkness there
The picture of its great despair!

Yet ever at the hour I feel
My lips in prophecy unseal.
Prince, priest, and Levite gather near,
And Salem's daughters haste to hear,
On Chebar's waste and alien shore,
The harp of Judah swept once more.
They listen, as in Babel's throng
The Chaldeans to the dancer's song,
Or wild Sabbeka's nightly play,
As careless and as vain as they.

And thus, O Prophet-bard of old,
Hast thou thy tale of sorrow told!
The same which earth's unwelcome seers
Have felt in all succeeding years.
Sport of the changeful multitude,
Nor calmly heard nor understood,
Their song has seemed a trick of art,
Their warnings but the actor's part,
With bonds, and scorn, and evil will,
The world requites its prophets still.
. . . .

Yet shrink not thou, whoe'er thou art,
For God's great purpose set apart,
Before whose far-discerning eyes,
The Future as the Present lies!

Beyond a narrow-bounded age
Stretches thy prophet-heritage,
Through Heaven's vast spaces angel-trod,
And through the eternal years of God!
Thy audience, worlds!—All things to be
The witness of the Truth in thee!

JOHN GREENLEAF WHITTIER

57

LEGEND OF IYOB THE UPRIGHT

(From *The Son of a Prophet*)

The mountains talk of Ben Rahah,
And the caves of Argob have their heroes;
Kenath and Batanah and Salkad exult,
They rejoice in their favorite sons.
But our lance is one, it is Uz of the fathers,
When we speak the name of Iyob.
He dwelt long ago in the south land:
Iyob the Upright, the prince of his people,
Rich in sons and daughters.
His oxen ploughed from desert to mountain,
His camels traded from sea to sea;
The wealth of a tribe his she-asses,
The clothing of a nation his sheep.
But men named him not for his wealth;
All knew him as Iyob the Upright.
He feared Eloah the God of his fathers,
The God of Esau, the son of Abraham.
With sacrifices he looked to the Maker of the heavens,

And sanctified his house with burnt-offerings.
When he came to the cities, he sat in the gates;
For he judged righteous judgment.
When he passed through the land there was joy;
For the poor were made rich by his bounty.
Of the sons of the East the greatest,
Of all he was best and most blessed:
Men said, "Be righteous and be as Iyob."
    Then a marvel:
In a day his riches took wings.
The Sabeans came from afar,
The swords of the bands of the Chaldeans.
Oxen and asses and camels were gone,
Snatched by the plunderers.
Fire fell from heaven;
The sheep were consumed at one offering.
One only escaped to bring each tale of disaster.
Then another came, telling a tale more awful:
"Thy sons and thy daughters were feasting together,
And now together they are not.
The house was crushed by the cyclone,
Its walls are now their tomb."
Then rose up Iyob the Upright,
And bowed before God and worshipped:
"Naked came I from my mother's womb,
And naked shall I return.
Eloah gave, Eloah hath taken;
Lo, I am thy servant, Eloah!"
  Again a blow, and men said,
"Can this be Iyob the Upright?"
With sore disease he was smitten:

A festering outcast he sat among the ashes.
Of the thousands who had waited his will,
His wife alone now served him.
Despairing, she understood not his trust:
"Renounce Eloah," she said, "and die."
"Shall we receive good from Eloah," he answered;
"And shall we not receive evil?"
   And yet once more he was crushed.
The multitude had fled with his wealth;
The contempt of the proud had come with his sores.
Yet he said, "I can bear it;
My true friends still trust me."
Then these friends appointed to meet him,
And came and sat down in his presence.
Eliphaz the seer came from Teman,
Bildad from Shuah, and Zophar from Naamah.
Seven days they sat and spake not,
Then they opened their mouths and—rebuked him:
His trusted friends, his last hope on earth, condemned him.
He had sinned and was hiding his evil;
Let him confess and return to Eloah.
But he knew himself Iyob the Upright,
And would none of their charges of evil.
Nay, but it must be; only guilt could bring suffering,
Could have brought such sudden destruction.
Let him pretend no more to be upright,
But repent that God might have mercy.
   In vain he protested innocence,
In vain he appealed to their mercy:

They were deaf to his cries.
He himself or Eloah who smote him,
The man or his Maker had done wickedness.
Should mortal man be more just than God?
Should a man be more pure than his Maker?
Then the bitterness of Iyob was utter:
But still he was Iyob the Upright.
He opened his mouth and spake:
"Though Eloah slay me, yet will I trust him;
I fear, I adore, I will not forsake him."
Lo, then a whirlwind, and the voice of Eloah!
"Behold Iyob, I have owned him;
He speaketh of me the thing that is right,
He loveth me, not mine; I accept him."
Then to Iyob was restored abundance,
And sons and daughters enriched him.
Again he was hailed the Prince of his people;
He is honored to all generations.

GEORGE ANSON JACKSON

58

JUDITH AND HOLOFERNES

(From *Judith*)

One cresset twinkled dimly in the tent
Of Holofernes, and Bagoas, his slave,
Lay prone across the matting at the door,
Drunk with the wine of slumber; but his lord
Slept not.
. . . .
"Go fetch me wine, and let my soul make cheer,
For I am sick with visions of the night.

Some strangest malady of breast and brain
Hath so unnerved me that a rustling leaf
Sets my pulse leaping. 'Tis a family flaw,
A flaw in men else flawless, this dark spell:
I do remember when my grandsire died,
He thought a lying Ethiop he had slain
Was strangling him; and, later, my own sire
Went mad with dreams the day before his death.
And I, too? Slave! go fetch me seas of wine,
That I may drown these fantasies—no, stay!
Ransack the camps for choicest flesh and fruit,
And spread a feast within my tent this night,
And hang the place with garlands of new flowers;
Then bid the Hebrew woman, yea or nay,
To banquet with us. As thou lov'st the light,
Bring her: and if indeed the gods have called,
The gods shall find me sitting at my feast
Consorting with a daughter of the gods!"
Thus Holofernes, turning on his heel
Impatiently; and straight Bagoas went
And spoiled the camps of viands for the feast,
And hung the place with flowers, as he was bid;
And seeing Judith's servant at the well,
Gave his lord's message, to which answer came:
"O what am I that should gainsay my lord?"

. . . .

"So soon!" thought Judith. "Flying pulse, be
    still!
O thou who lovest Israel, give me strength
And cunning such as never woman had,
That my deceit may be his stripe and scar,
My kisses his destruction. This for thee,

My city, Bethûlia, this for thee!"
And thrice that day she prayed within her heart,
Bowed down among the cushions of the tent
In shame and wretchedness; and thus she prayed:
"O save me from him, Lord! but save me most
From mine own sinful self."

  .   .   .   .

Half seen behind the forehead of a crag
The evening-star grew sharp against the dusk,
As Judith lingered by the curtained door
Of her pavilion, waiting for Bagoas:
Erewhile he came, and led her to the tent
Of Holofernes; and she entered in,
And knelt before him in the cresset's glare
Demurely, like a slave-girl at the feet
Of her new master, while the modest blood
Makes protest to the eyelids; and he leaned
Graciously over her, and bade her rise
And sit beside him on the leopard-skins.
But Judith would not, yet with gentlest grace
Would not; and partly to conceal her blush,
Partly to quell the riot in her breast,
She turned, and wrapt her in her fleecy scarf,
And stood aloof, nor looked as one that breathed,
But rather like some jewelled deity
Taken by a conqueror from its sacred niche,
And placed among the trappings of his tent—
So pure was Judith.   For a moment's space
She stood, then stealing softly to his side,
Knelt down by him, and with uplifted face,
Whereon the red rose blossomed with the white:

"This night, my lord, no other slave than I
Shall wait on thee with fruits and flowers and wine.
So subtle am I, I shall know thy wish
Ere thou canst speak it. Let Bagoas go
Among his people: let me wait and serve,
More happy as thy handmaid than thy guest."

. . . .

So Judith served and Holofernes drank,
Until the lamps that glimmered round the tent
In mad processions danced before his gaze.

. . . .

And once he thought the Hebrew woman sang
A wine song, touching on a certain king
Who, dying of strange sickness, drank, and past
Beyond the touch of mortal agony—
A vague tradition of the cunning sprite
That dwells within the circle of the grape.

. . . .

"A potent medicine for kings and men,"
Thus Holofernes, "he was wise to drink;
Be thou as wise, fair Judith." As he spoke,
He stoopt to kiss the treacherous soft hand
That rested like a snowflake on his arm,
But stooping reeled, and from the place he sat
Toppled, and fell among the leopard-skins;
There lay, nor stirred; and ere ten beats of heart,
The tawny giant slumbered. . . . .
. . . . . With quick breath
Judith blew out the tapers, all save one,
And from his twisted girdle loosed the sword,
And grasping the huge hilt with her two hands,
Thrice smote the Prince of Assur as he lay;

Thrice on his neck she smote him as he lay,
And from the brawny shoulders rolled the head
Winking and ghastly in the cresset's light ;
Which done, she fled into the yawning dark,
There met her maid, who, stealing to the tent,
Pulled down the crimson arras on the corse,
And in her mantle wrapped the brazen head
And brought it with her ;   .   .   .   .
    .   .   .   .   but outside the camp
Terror seized on them and they fled like wraiths
Through the hushed midnight into the black woods,
Where from gnarled roots and ancient, palsied trees
Dread shapes, upstarting, clutched at them ; and once,
A nameless bird in branches overhead
Screeched, and the blood grew cold about their hearts.
By mouldy caves, the hooded viper's haunt,
Down perilous steeps, and through the desolate gorge,
Onward they flew with madly streaming hair,
Bearing their hideous burden, till at last,
Wild with the pregnant horrors of the night,
They dashed themselves against the City's gate.
       .   .   .   .

So by God's grace and this one woman's hand,
The tombs and temples of the just were saved ;
And evermore throughout fair Israel
The name of Judith meant all noblest things
In thought and deed ; and Judith's life was rich
With that content the world takes not away.

And far-off kings enamored of her fame,
Bluff princes, dwellers by the salt sea-sands,
Sent caskets most laboriously carved
Of ivory, and papyrus scrolls, whereon
Was writ their passion; then themselves did come
With spicy caravans, in purple state,
To seek regard from her imperial eyes.
But she remained unwed, and to the end
Walked with the angels in her widow's weeds.

THOMAS BAILEY ALDRICH

59
THE PRAYER OF MARDOCHEUS

(Esther [Apocrypha] xiii)

O Lord, my Lord, That art the King of might,
  Within Whose power all things their being have!
Who may withstand that liveth in Thy sight,
  If Thou Thy chosen Israel wilt save?
    For Thou hast made the earth and heaven above,
    And all things else that in the same do move.

Thou madest all things, and they are all Thine own,
  And there is none that may resist Thy will:
Thou know'st all things, and this of Thee is known,
  I did not erst for malice nor for ill,
    Presumption nor vain glory else at all,
    Come nor bow down unto proud Haman's call.

I could have been content for Israel's sake
To kiss the soles even of his very feet,
But that I would not man's vain honour take
Before God's glory, being so unmeet,
 And would not worship none, O Lord, but
  Thee !
 And not of pride, as Thou Thyself dost see.

Therefore, O Lord, my God and heavenly King,
Have mercy on the people Thou hast bought !
For they imagine and devise the thing
How to destroy and bring us unto nought,
 Thine heritance, which Thou so long hast
  fed,
 And out so far from Egypt-land hast led.

O hear my prayer, and mercy do extend
Upon Thy portion of inheritance !
For sorrow now some joy and solace send,
That we may live Thy glory to advance ;
 And suffer not their mouths shut up, O
  Lord,
 Which still Thy Name with praises do
  record !
MICHAEL DRAYTON

60

NEHEMIAH

(From *Bible Characters*)

Ninety-two years after the edict of Cyrus, Single-heart stepped upon the scene. He was a Jew, born probably in Persia, and rose, in spite of his

origin, by rare ability, to a high place in the service
of Artaxerxes. His title was cup-bearer; but all
such titles are misleading. He was a statesman
and a courtier, and it was only one of his duties to
taste the wine before he poured out for the king,
and so secure him at his own risk against poison.
This royal favorite, bred in soft Persia and lodged
in those earthly paradises, the summer palace and
winter palace of his monarch, had yet "Jerusalem
written on his heart."

. . . .

Singleheart, better known as Nehemiah, was
leading a life of delights with the king at Shushan,
when Hanani, a pious Jew, who had gone with a
company to visit Jerusalem, returned from that
journey. Nehemiah questioned him eagerly about
their city and countrymen.

Then Hanani and his fellows hung their heads,
and told Nehemiah that the remnant of the captivity in that land were in great affliction and
reproach; the wall of Jerusalem, also, was broken
down, and the gates burned with fire.

See now how Jerusalem was beloved by her exiled
sons! Born, bred, and thriving in soft, seductive
Persia, the true-hearted Jew Nehemiah was struck
down directly by these words. He who had a
right to stand on the steps of the greatest throne
in the world sat down upon the ground, and fasted
and wept and prayed before the God of heaven;
and this was his confession and his prayer: "O
Lord God of heaven, we have dealt very corruptly
against thee, and have not kept the commandments,

nor the statutes, nor the judgments, which thou commandedst thy servant Moses. Remember, I beseech thee, the word that thou commandedst thy servant Moses, saying, If ye transgress, I will scatter you abroad among the nations: but if ye turn unto me, and keep my commandments, and do them; though there were of you cast out unto the uttermost part of the heaven, yet will I gather them from thence, and will bring them unto the place that I have chosen to set my name there. . . .

Public men are slaves as well as masters, their consciences seldom their own, their time never. Neither their pleasures nor their griefs can be long indulged. The bereaved statesman is not allowed to be quiet and to mourn; he must leave the new grave and the desolate home for his arena, sometimes must even take part in a public festivity with a bleeding heart. This very thing befell Nehemiah. . . . .

Great Artaxerxes gave a superb banquet to his nobility: the queen was there—no every-day event. . . . Gold plate by the ton, gorgeous silk dresses of every hue, marble pillars, fountains, music, lights to turn night into day, slaves, sultanas, courtiers resplendent as stars, and all worshipping their sun Artaxerxes. . . . .

It was Singleheart's duty to present the cup to this earthly divinity. So he took up the golden goblet, filled it ceremoniously, and offered it with a deep obeisance, as he had often done before; but now for the first time with a sorrowful face.

This was so strange a thing in him, or indeed in

any courtier, that the king noticed it at once; even as he took the cup his eye dwelt on this sad face, and he said directly, "Why is your countenance sad?"

Nehemiah was too much taken aback to reply. The king questioned him again. "You are not sick?"

Still no reply.

"This is sorrow, and nothing else."

Then Nehemiah was sore afraid, and I will tell you why. His life was in danger. Even a modern autocrat like Louis XIV expected everybody's face to shine if he did but appear, and how much more an Artaxerxes! . . . .

But though Nehemiah felt his danger, yet the king's actual words were not menacing, and the courtier found courage to tell the simple truth. He salaamed down to the ground. "Let the king live forever!" After this propitiatory formula he replied, "Why should not my countenance be sad, when the city, the place of my fathers' sepulchres, lieth waste, and its gates are burned with fire?"

These are brave words, and can be read aggressively; only that is not how Nehemiah spoke them. It was his to propitiate, not to offend, and his tones were broken-hearted and appealing, not contumacious.

Then Nehemiah set us all an example. He did not answer the king out of his own head, and pray for wisdom six hours afterwards, because it was bed-time. He prayed standing on the spot, and, like a skilful gunner, shot the occasion flying.

Strengthened by ejaculatory prayer, the soul's best weapon, he said, "If it please the king, and if thy servant has found favor in thy sight, pray send me to Judah, unto the city of my fathers' sepulchres, that I may rebuild it."

The king's answer was rather favorable. He was unwilling to lose a good servant forever, and asked him how long he wished to be away; but this was as much as to say he should go upon conditions.

When that one point was settled, and leave of absence conceded, Nehemiah got bolder and bolder. He asked for passports where needed, and an order on Asaph for timber, etc. The liberal monarch granted all, and even volunteered a cavalry escort to see him safe to the end of that long and perilous journey. In recording the first of these petitions the autobiographer, Nehemiah, suddenly informs us that the queen was sitting by the king's side. This looks as if he connected her somehow in his own mind with his petition and the king's bounty, and rather favors the notion that she was the famous Esther, and sympathized then and there with her sad countryman by look or gesture.

So Singleheart left the lap of luxury and rode with his escort from Shushan to Jerusalem. . . .

He reached Jerusalem, . . . and on the third day, in the middle of the night, he rose and took with him, not his Persian escort to make a clatter of hoofs and a parade, but a few trusty men on foot, and even to them he did not reveal "What God had put into his heart to do at Jerusalem." So with his secret locked at present in his breast, he passed out by the gate of the valley and round the city, and under the silver light of the moon and stars viewed the clean gaps, the burned fragments of the gates, and the jagged breaches in the walls of the holy city. . . . .

Fresh from that starlight picture Nehemiah went to the Jewish nobles, priests and princes, showed the powers he held under the hand of Artaxerxes, and urged them to rebuild the walls and revive the national glory. He has not told us what he said; but it is clear he found words of rare eloquence; for they all caught fire directly, and cried out, "Let us rise and build."

CHARLES READE

61

NEHEMIAH, REFORMER

(From *Bible Characters*)

It is clear from Nehemiah's own account that intermarriage with heathen, and other abuses, proved too strong for Ezra in the long run. Nehemiah found this malpractice and many others at Jerusalem, . . . [and] set himself to reform this, but not this alone. He was not a better, but a greater, man than Ezra, and made wiser reforms, and kept them alive, which Ezra failed to do.

One thing that shocked him much was the usurious practices of the wealthier Jews, and their cruelty in selling their poor debtors into bondage. "What!" said he, "we have redeemed our brethren that were sold unto the heathen, and will ye sell your brethren?" and they found nothing to answer. Then he reminded them he had power to levy large exactions upon *them*, and besought them to imitate his moderation.

Such was the power of his example, and his remonstrances that he actually induced the creditors to restore to the ruined debtors their houses, vineyards, and olive-yards, and a little of the forfeited produce to keep them alive through the famine.

When the relenting creditors had bound themselves to this by oath, he took his tunic in both hands and shook it, and said, "May God so shake out every man from his house and from his labor who performeth not this promise."

This was a master-stroke, and shows the man of genius. Such appeals to the senses as well as to the conscience take the whole mind by assault, and fix the matter forever in the memory. His hearers cried "Amen" and praised the Lord and—kept their promises. . . . .

Both priests and laymen had become loose in observing the Sabbath day. He found Jews treading the wine-presses, gathering in the harvests, and trading on the Sabbath day, and men of Tyre bringing fish and other wares into the markets of the city.

He treated natives and aliens alike, stopped the home trade, and closed the gates of the city against the Tyrians.

But the Tyrians were hard to deal with; they lodged outside the wall, and offered their wares outside.

"Do that again," said Nehemiah, "and I will lay hands on you." This frightened them away for good.

Then came his worst trouble, the persistent intermarriage with heathen.

Ezra had withstood this for years in vain. Nehemiah had combated it with partial success; yet now Nehemiah found Jews who had married wives of Ashdod, Ammon, and Moab, and their children could not speak Hebrew, but naturally spoke their mother-tongue.

Then he came out in a new character. He contended with them, and cursed them, and smote certain of them, and plucked off their hair, and made them swear by God not to give their daughters to heathen husbands nor their sons to heathen wives again.

After this outburst of impassioned zeal, which at first takes the student of his mind a little by surprise, he returned to his grave character, and reasoned the matter with those he had terrified into submission.

"What Jew," said he, "was ever so wise, so great, so beloved of God, as King Solomon? Yet outlandish women could make even him sin against God, and commit idolatry."

Nehemiah prevailed, and there is reason to believe that idolatry received its death-blow under his rule.

He ends his brief but noble record with his favorite prayer, "Remember me, O my God, for good." That prayer has long been granted. But

the children of God on earth have not seen all his
value. Do but enumerate the various parts he
played, the distinct virtues he showed, the strokes
of genius he extemporized—and all to serve, not
himself, but his country and his God. Faithful
courtier, yet true patriot; child of luxury, yet.
patient of hardship; inventive builder, impromptu
general, astute politician, high-spirited gentleman,
inspired orator, resolute reformer—born leader of
men, yet humble before God.

CHARLES READE

62

MÁHALA AND HER SEVEN SONS

(From *Judas Maccabæus*)

Act II, Scene I

THE MOTHER

Be strong, my heart! Break not till they are dead,
All, all my Seven Sons; then burst asunder,
And let this tortured and tormented soul
Leap and rush out like water through the shards
Of earthen vessels broken at a well.

. . . .

I do not murmur, nay, I thank thee, God,
That I and mine have not been deemed unworthy
To suffer for thy sake, and for thy law,
And for the many sins of Israel.
Hark! I can hear within the sound of scourges!
I feel them more than ye do, O my sons!

But cannot come to you. I, who was wont
To wake at night at the least cry ye made,
To whom ye ran at every slightest hurt, —
I cannot take you now into my lap
And soothe your pain, but God will take you all
Into his pitying arms, and comfort you,
And give you rest.

         A VOICE (*within*)

               What wouldst thou ask of us?
Ready are we to die, but we will never
Transgress the law and customs of our fathers.

         THE MOTHER

It is the voice of my first-born! O brave
And noble boy! Thou hast the privilege
Of dying first, as thou wast born the first.

         THE SAME VOICE (*within*)

God looketh on us, and hath comfort in us;
As Moses in his song of old declared,
He in his servants shall be comforted.

         THE MOTHER

I knew thou wouldst not fail!—He speaks no more,
He is beyond all pain!

         ANTIOCHUS (*within*)

               If thou eat not
Thou shalt be tortured throughout all the members
Of thy whole body. Wilt thou eat then?

         SECOND VOICE (*within*)
                       No.

THE MOTHER

It is Adaiah's voice. I tremble for him.
I know his nature, devious as the wind,
And swift to change, gentle and yielding always,
Be steadfast, O my son!

THE SAME VOICE (*within*)

       Thou, like a fury,
Takest us from this present life, but God
Who rules the world, shall raise us up again
Into life everlasting.

THE MOTHER

       God, I thank thee
That thou hast breathed into that timid heart
Courage to die for thee. O my Adaiah,
Witness of God! if thou for whom I feared
Canst thus encounter death, I need not fear;
The others will not shrink.

THIRD VOICE (*within*)

       Behold these hands
Held out to thee, O King Antiochus,
Not to implore thy mercy, but to show
That I despise them. He who gave them to me—
Will give them back again.

THE MOTHER

       O Avilan,
It is thy voice. For the last time I hear it;
For the last time on earth, but not the last.
To death it bids defiance and to torture.
It sounds to me as from another world,

And makes the petty miseries of this
Seem unto me as naught, and less than naught.
Farewell, my Avilan; nay, I should say
Welcome, my Avilan; for I am dead
Before thee. I am waiting for the others.
Why do they linger?

        FOURTH VOICE (*within*)
                  It is good, O King,
Being put to death by men, to look for hope
From God, to be raised up again by him.
But thou—no resurrection shalt thou have
To life hereafter.

        THE MOTHER
                Four! already four!
Three are still living; nay, they all are living,
Half here, half there. Make haste, Antiochus,
To reunite us; for the sword that cleaves
These miserable bodies makes a door
Through which our souls, impatient of release,
Rush to each other's arms.

        FIFTH VOICE (*within*)
                  Thou hast the power;
Thou doest what thou wilt. Abide awhile,
And thou shalt see the power of God, and how
He will torment thee and thy seed.

        THE MOTHER
                    O hasten;
Why dost thou pause? Thou who hast slain already
So many Hebrew women, and hast hung
Their murdered infants round their necks, slay
    me,

For I too am a woman, and these boys
Are mine. Make haste to slay us all,
And hang my lifeless babes about my neck.

   SIXTH VOICE (*within*)
Think not, Antiochus, that takest in hand
To strive against the God of Israel,
Thou shalt escape unpunished, for his wrath
Shall overtake thee and thy bloody house.

   THE MOTHER
One more, my Sirion, and then all is ended.
Having put all to bed, then in my turn
I will lie down and sleep as sound as they.
My Sirion, my youngest, best beloved!
And those bright golden locks, that I so oft
Have curled about these fingers, even now
Are foul with blood and dust, like a lamb's fleece,
Slain in the shambles.—Not a sound I hear.
This silence is more terrible to me
Than any sound, than any cry of pain,
That might escape the lips of one who dies.
Doth his heart fail him? Doth he fall away
In the last hour from God? O Sirion, Sirion,
Art thou afraid? I do not hear thy voice.
Die as thy brothers died. Thou must not live!

Scene II

THE MOTHER; ANTIOCHUS; SIRION.

   THE MOTHER
Are they all dead?

ANTIOCHUS

                Of all thy Seven Sons
One only lives. Behold them where they lie!
How dost thou like this picture?

THE MOTHER

                    God in heaven!
Can a man do such deeds, and yet not die
By the recoil of his own wickedness?
Ye murdered, bleeding, mutilated bodies
That were my children once, and still are mine,
I cannot watch o'er you as Rizpah watched
In sackcloth o'er the seven sons of Saul,
Till water drop upon you out of heaven
And wash this blood away! I cannot mourn
As she, the daughter of Aiah, mourned the dead,
From the beginning of the barley-harvest
Until the autumn rains, and suffered not
The birds of air to rest on them by day,
Nor the wild beasts by night. For ye have died
A better death, a death so full of life
That I ought rather to rejoice than mourn.—
Wherefore art thou not dead, O Sirion?
Wherefore art thou the only living thing
Among thy brothers dead! Art thou afraid?

ANTIOCHUS

O woman, I have spared him for thy sake,
For he is fair to look upon and comely;
And I have sworn to him by all the gods,
That I would crown his life with joy and honor,
Heap treasures on him, luxuries, delights,

Make him my friend and keeper of my secrets,
If he would turn from your Mosaic Law
And be as we are; but he will not listen.

THE MOTHER

My noble Sirion.

ANTIOCHUS

Therefore I beseech thee,
Who art his mother, thou wouldst speak with him,
And wouldst persuade him. I am sick of blood.

THE MOTHER

Yea, I will speak with him and will persuade him.
O Sirion, my son! have pity on me,
On me that bare thee, and that gave thee suck
And fed and nourished thee, and brought thee up
With the dear trouble of a mother's care
Unto this age. Look on the heavens above thee,
And on the earth and all that is therein;
Consider that God made them out of things
That were not; and that likewise in this manner
Mankind was made. Then fear not this tormentor;
But, being worthy of thy brethren, take
Thy death as they did, that I may receive thee
Again in mercy with them.

ANTIOCHUS

I am mocked,
Yea, I am laughed to scorn.

SIRION

Whom wait ye for?
Never will I obey the King's commandment,

But the commandment of the ancient Law,
That was by Moses given unto our fathers.
And thou, O godless man, that of all others
Art the most wicked, be not lifted up,
Nor puffed up with uncertain hopes, uplifting
Thy hand against the servants of the Lord,
For thou hast not escaped the righteous judgment
Of the Almighty God, who seeth all things!

ANTIOCHUS

He is no God of mine: I fear him not.

SIRION

My brothers, who have suffered a brief pain,
Are dead; but thou, Antiochus, shalt suffer
The punishment of pride. I offer up
My body and my life, beseeching God
That he would speedily be merciful
Unto our nation; and that thou by plagues
Mysterious and by torments mayest confess
That He alone is God.

ANTIOCHUS

                   Ye both shall perish
By torments worse than any that your God,
Here or hereafter, hath in store for me.

THE MOTHER

My Sirion, I am proud of thee.

ANTIOCHUS

                       Be silent!
Go to thy bed of torture in yon chamber,
Where lie so many sleepers, heartless mother!

Thy footsteps will not wake them, nor thy voice,
Nor wilt thou hear, amid thy troubled dreams,
Thy children crying for thee in the night!

THE MOTHER

O Death, that stretchest thy white hands to me,
I fear them not, but press them to my lips,
That are as white as thine; for I am Death,
Nay, am the mother of Death, seeing these sons
All lying lifeless.—Kiss me, Sirion.

H. W. LONGFELLOW

63
JUDAS MACCABÆUS

(From *Judas Maccabæus*)

Act III

The Battle-field of Beth-Horon

Scene I—JUDAS MACCABÆUS *in armor before his tent.*

JUDAS

The trumpets sound; the echoes of the mountains
Answer them, as the Sabbath morning breaks
Over Beth-horon and its battle-field,
Where the great captain of the hosts of God,
A slave brought up in the brick-fields of Egypt,
O'ercame the Amorites. There was no day
Like that, before or after it, nor shall be.
The sun stood still; the hammers of the hail
Beat on their harness; and the captains set

Their weary feet upon the necks of kings,
As I will upon thine, Antiochus,
Thou man of blood! Behold the rising sun
Strikes on the golden letters of my banner,
Be Elohim Yehovah! Who is like
To thee, O Lord, among the gods?—Alas!
I am not Joshua, I cannot say,
" Sun, stand thou still on Gibeon, and thou Moon,
In Ajalon!" Nor am I one who wastes
The fateful time in useless lamentation;
But one who bears his life upon his hand
To lose it or to save it, as may best
Serve the designs of Him who giveth life.

SCENE II—JUDAS MACCABÆUS; JEWISH FUGITIVES

JUDAS

Who and what are ye, that with furtive steps
Steal in among our tents?

FUGITIVES

                O Maccabæus,
Outcasts are we, and fugitives as thou art,
Jews of Jerusalem, that have escaped
From the polluted city, and from death.

JUDAS

None can escape from death. Say that ye come
To die for Israel, and ye are welcome.
What tidings bring ye?

FUGITIVES

           Tidings of despair.
The Temple is laid waste; the precious vessels,

Censers of gold, vials and veils and crowns,
And golden ornaments, and hidden treasures,
Have all been taken from it, and the Gentiles
With revelling and with riot fill its courts.
 . . . .

JUDAS

All this I knew before.

FUGITIVES

        Upon the altar
Are things profane, things by the law forbidden;
Nor can we keep our Sabbaths or our Feasts,
But on the festival of Dionysus
Must walk in their processions, bearing ivy
To crown a drunken god.

JUDAS

       This too I know,
But tell me of the Jews. How fare the Jews?

FUGITIVES

The coming of this mischief hath been sore
And grievous to the people. All the land
Is full of lamentation and of mourning.
The Princes and the Elders weep and wail;
The young men and the maidens are made feeble;
The beauty of the women hath been changed.

JUDAS

And are there none to die for Israel?
'Tis not enough to mourn. Breastplate and harness
Are better things than sackcloth. Let the women
Lament for Israel; the men should die.

FUGITIVES

Both men and women die; old men and young;
Old Eleazer died; and Máhala
With all her Seven Sons.

JUDAS

Antiochus,
At every step thou takest there is left
A bloody footprint in the street, by which
The avenging wrath of God will track thee out!
It is enough. Go to the sutler's tents:
Those of you who are men, put on such armor
As ye may find; those of you who are women,
Buckle that armor on; and for a watchword
Whisper, or cry aloud, "The Help of God."

H. W. LONGFELLOW

64

THE BATTLE OF BETH-HORON

(From *Judas Maccabæus*)

SCENE IV —JUDAS MACCABÆUS; CAPTAINS AND SOLDIERS

JUDAS

The hour is come. Gather the host together
For battle. Lo, with trumpets and with songs
The army of Nicanor comes against us.
Go forth to meet them, praying in your hearts,
And fighting with your hands.

CAPTAINS

Look forth and see!
The morning sun is shining on their shields
Of gold and brass; the mountains glisten with
  them,
And shine like lamps. And we who are so few
And poorly armed, and ready to faint with fasting,
How shall we fight against this multitude?

JUDAS

The victory of a battle standeth not
In multitudes, but in the strength that cometh
From heaven above. The Lord forbid that I
Should do this thing, and flee away from them.
Nay if our hour be come, then let us die;
Let us not stain our honor.

CAPTAINS

'Tis the Sabbath.
Wilt thou fight on the Sabbath, Maccabæus?

JUDAS

Ay; when I fight the battles of the Lord,
I fight them on his day, as on all others.
Have ye forgotten certain fugitives
That fled once to these hills, and hid themselves
In caves? How their pursuers camped against them
Upon the Seventh Day, and challenged them?
And how they answered not, nor cast a stone,
Nor stopped the places where they lay concealed,
But meekly perished with their wives and children,
Even to the number of a thousand souls?

We who are fighting for our laws and lives
Will not so perish.

    CAPTAINS

      Lead us to the battle!

    JUDAS

And let our watchword be, "The Help of God!"
Last night I dreamed a dream; and in my vision
Beheld Onias, our High Priest of old,
Who holding up his hands prayed for the Jews.
This done, in the like manner there appeared
An old man, and exceeding glorious,
With hoary hair, and of a wonderful
And excellent majesty. And Onias said:
"This is a lover of the Jews, who prayeth
Much for the people and the Holy City,—
God's prophet Jeremias." And the prophet
Held forth his right hand and gave unto me
A sword of gold; and giving it he said:
"Take thou this holy sword, a gift from God,
And with it thou shalt wound thine adversaries."

    CAPTAINS

The Lord is with us!

    JUDAS

      Hark! I hear the trumpets
Sound from Beth-horon; from the battle-field
Of Joshua, where he smote the Amorites,
Smote the Five Kings of Eglon, and of Jarmuth,
Of Hebron, Lachish, and Jerusalem,

As we to-day will smite Nicanor's hosts,
And leave a memory of great deeds behind us.

CAPTAINS AND SOLDIERS

The Help of God!

JUDAS

Be Elohim Yehovah!
Lord, thou didst send thine Angel in the time
Of Ezekias, King of Israel,
And in the armies of Sennacherib
Didst slay a hundred fourscore and five thousand.
Wherefore, O Lord of heaven, now also send
Before us a good angel for a fear,
And through the might of thy right arm let those
Be stricken with terror that have come this day
Against thy holy people to blaspheme!

H. W. LONGFELLOW

65

THE PHARISEES

(From *Women of Israel*)

To obtain a just and impartial estimate of the real character, intentions, and bearings of the body, known as the Pharisees, is to the Hebrew of the present day almost impossible. The Jew, whose mind and heart have been guided by his Talmudical studies, cannot fail to regard them with the deepest veneration and love;—the Jew, who has known them only through the medium of Gentile writers, must unconsciously imbibe a portion of their feeling, and perhaps regard them only as superstitious zealots, following the letter of the law, but not its spirit. The allusions to the Pharisees, in the book which Gentiles believe divine, and the subsequent explanations in their various commentaries, cannot fail to engender this spirit. But the Hebrew should guard against imbibing it, because the view is false in many of its bearings. It is very difficult, when we only possess histories written by Gentiles in a liberal and friendly spirit, and containing so much with which we can fully sympathize, to realize that on some points as Hebrews, our opinions must form themselves, and not be guided by those of the historian. The Pharisees is one of these—on which we must reflect and exercise our own judgment. The Rabbinical historian would unhesitatingly pronounce them saints, as little less holy or inspired than the prophets themselves;—the Gentiles, as cruel, prejudiced bigots, hiding the most fearful vices under the mask of extremest sanctity. Both are probably wrong. The Pharisees were but men, liable to all the failings of humanity; but their religion, even if carried beyond the law, was honest and sincere. The laxity and indifference of the multitude compelled a greater degree of strictness; they were forced to raise around them a wall of exclusiveness, lest they too should fall. They beheld the awful evils creeping steadily amidst all ranks, and was it strange that they should have encouraged an unsocial spirit, and held themselves aloof? They beheld foreign manners and customs destroying the nationality of their people and land; that the law of their God, which they justly held supreme, was disregarded; and was it unnatural that they should seclude themselves, proud of their spiritual superiority—or that their attachment to their land and Temple should increase in passionate intensity, as they beheld it so often trampled upon and desecrated by foreigners? That a want of charity, of humility, of forbearance, marked their religion, might be; nay, in that terrible period it could scarcely be otherwise. Party spirit even then had dried up the channels of social affection, and the spirit of love and meekness which the religion of Moses taught, could not be realized in the popular tumults and crimes forever raging round them. Individuals there were, no doubt, combining the pure spirit and loving mind with the outward ceremonial; but in this brief sketch we can only generalize. Still, spite of their faults—spite of the too rigid, too exclusive notions, which, if indeed they had existence, originated simply from the fear of being too lax, and sharing the indifference and infidelity of too many of their fellows, the Pharisees must be regarded with veneration as the preservers of the law.

GRACE AGUILAR

66

LINES FOR THE NINTH OF AB

Isaiah xl. 1.—נחמו נחמו עמי יאמר אלהיכם

Shall I sorrow, oh desolate city,
    For thy beauty and glory o'erthrown?
Shall I sing the dread day of destruction,
    When thy sins thou didst dearly atone?
When the Lord from the place He had chosen
    In anger withdrew His great name,
And its treasures were spoiled by the stranger,
    Its holiness given to shame—
When the shrieks of the daughters of Zion
    Sad echo'd the shouts of the foe,
And thy streets, ravished City, ran crimson
    With the blood of thy sons, lying low—
When the sceptre departed from Judah,
    From Levi his birthright was riven,
And the people of God were led captive
    Forsaken of earth and of Heaven!

Or shall I rejoice in the beauty
    And glory, again to be thine,
When thy youth's loving Bridegroom shall ransom
    His promise of comfort divine—
When the rites of thy temple new-builded
    With God shall find grace, as of old,
And monarchs shall hasten with offerings
    Of incense and jewels and gold?
In musical chorus, thy daughters
    Shall echo the Levite's glad song,

And thy gates night and day shall stand open
  For the pilgrims that thitherward throng
For the sceptre returneth to David,
  The mitre to Aaron's proud line :
And neighbor shall welcome his neighbor
  To the shadow of fig-tree and vine!

Like Akiba, who laugh'd when the foxes
  Ran out from the Holiest place,
Saying : "True were the warnings of evil
  And true is the promise of grace,"
My thoughts on this day of sad memories
  Turn not back to the past in despair,
But forward, in hope, to the future
  Where visions of glory shine fair!
When I read in the book of the prophet
  Who voiced fallen Zion's distress,
I seek not alone words of grieving,
  But these rarer, that comfort and bless :
"Hear the word of the Lord, oh ye nations,
  In the isles afar-off be it told ;
Who dispersed, will again gather Israel,
  And keep, as a shepherd his fold!"

SOLOMON SOLIS-COHEN

67

THE WILD GAZELLE

The wild gazelle on Judah's hills
  Exulting yet may bound,
And drink from all the living rills
  That gush on holy ground;

Its airy step and glorious eye
May glance in tameless transport by:—

A step as fleet, an eye more bright,
    Hath Judah witness'd there;
And o'er her scenes of lost delight
    Inhabitants more fair.
The cedars wave on Lebanon,
But Judah's statelier maids are gone!

More blest each palm that shades those plains
    Than Israel's scattered race:
For, taking root, it there remains
    In solitary grace:
It cannot quit its place of birth,
It will not live in other earth.

But we must wander witheringly,
    In other lands to die;
And where our fathers' ashes be,
    Our own may never lie:
Our temple hath not left a stone,
And Mockery sits on Salem's throne.

LORD BYRON

68

OZAIR THE JEW

What time fair Zion was given to sword and flame,
Ozair the Jew upon his camel came
Over those hills which ring the sea of Lot,
So that one footstep and—ye see her not,

And then another—and the city comes
Full upon view with all her milk-white domes.
But the Chaldean now had spoiled the place,
And desolate and waste was Zion's face,
Her proud abodes unpeopled, and her ways
Heaped with charred beams and lintels. Ozair says,
"O Lord! who promised to Jerusalem
Comfort and peace; and for her sons, to them
A glad return, how shall Thy word be kept
When fire and steel over these roofs have swept,
And she, that was a queen, lies dead and black,
A smoking ruin, where the jackals pack?
A hundred years were not enough to give
Life back to Zion! Can she ever live?"

But while he spake, the Angel of the Lord
Laid on his doubting front a fiery sword,
And Ozair in that lonely desert spot
Fell prone, and lay—breathing and moving not—
One hundred years, while the great world rolled on,
And Zion rose, and mighty deeds were done.
And when the hundred years were flown, God said,
"Awake, Ozair! how long hast tarriëd,
Thinkest thou, here?" Ozair replied, " A day,
Perchance, or half." The awful Voice said, "Nay!
But look upon thy camel." Of that beast
Naught save white bones was left; no sign, the least,
Of flesh, or hair, or hide; the desert grass
Was matted o'er its shanks, and roots did pass

From a gnarled fig-tree through the eye-pits twain,
And in and out its ribs grew the vervain.
But 'mid the moulderings of its saddle-bags
And crimson carpet, withered into rags,
A basket, full of new picked dates, stood there
Beside a cruise of water, standing where
He set them fresh, twice fifty years ago;
And all the dates were golden with the glow
Of yestreen's sunset, and the cruise's rim
Sparkled with water to the very brim.
"Ozair!" the awful Voice spake, "look on these!
He maketh and unmaketh what shall please;
Saves or destroys, restores or casts away;
And centuries to Him are as a day;
And cities all as easy to revive
As this thy camel here, which now shall live."
Thereon the skull and bones together crept
From tangled weed and sand where they had slept;
The hide and hair came, and the flesh filled in,
The eyes returned their hollow pits within,
The saddle-bags upon its haunches hung,
The carpet on the saddle-horns was flung,
The nose-rope from the muzzle fell. The beast
Rose from its knees, and would have made to feast
On the green herbage where its bones had lain,
But that it heard bells of a caravan
Coming from Kedron, and with glad cry roared.
Then Ozair looked, and saw newly restored
Zion's fair walls and temples, and a crowd
Of citizens and traffic rich and loud
In her white streets, and knew time should not be
Reckoned 'gainst Him who hath eternity.

EDWIN ARNOLD

69
BAR KOCHBA

Weep, Israel! your tardy meed outpour
    Of grateful homage on his fallen head,
That never coronal of triumph wore,
    Untombed, dishonored, and unchapleted.
If Victory makes the hero, raw Success
    The stamp of virtue, unremembered
Be then the desperate strife, the storm and stress
    Of the last Warrior Jew. But if the man
Who dies for freedom, loving all things less,
    Against world-legions, mustering his poor clan;
The weak, the wronged, the miserable, to send
    Their death-cry's protest through the ages' span—
If such an one be worthy, ye shall lend
    Eternal thanks to him, eternal praise.
Nobler the conquered than the conqueror's end!

                    EMMA LAZARUS

70
IN EXILE

(Tenth Century. From *Synagogale Poesie des Mittelalters*, by Leopold Zunz)

Weary and long are the years,
    Sorrow grows more and more;
Scarcely we rest from our fears,
    Our trouble never is o'er.
All the seasons pass on,
    No sign is seen in the sky;

Each ends as each has begun,
 The ages darkly glide by ;
And the grief is harder to bear,
 Old sorrow in newest array.
I dreamt that Redemption was near,
 I saw the dawn of its day ;
Yet still the troubles remain,
 Still, though they swore it would come ;
And they fix new seasons again,
 And they tell us of glory and home.
So the days of the exile glide on,
 In dreams, delusion, and woe,
"To-day or to-morrow the sun
 Will gladden all hearts with its glow ;"
And the faithful count up the days,
 Tell out their tale and are glad ;
But none of us knoweth Thy ways ;
 Vain yearning maketh us sad.

RABBI JOSEPH
Translation from the German by E. H. Plumptre

71

THE FIRST CRUSADE

(Mayence—from *Synagogale Poesie des Mittelalters*, by Leopold Zunz)

Yes, they slay us and they smite,
Vex our souls with sore affright ;
All the closer cleave we, Lord,
To Thine everlasting word.
Not a word of all their Mass
Shall our lips in homage pass ;

Though they curse, and bind, and kill,
The living God is with us still.
Yes, they fain would make us now,
Baptized, at Baal's altars bow;
On their raiment, wrought with gold,
See the sign we hateful hold;
And, with words of foulest shame
They outrage, Lord, the holiest Name:
We still are Thine, though limbs are torn;
Better death than life forsworn.
Noblest matrons seek for death,
Rob their children of their breath;
Fathers, in their fiery zeal,
Slay their sons with murderous steel,
And in heat of holiest strife,
For love of·Thee, spare not their life.
The fair and young lie down to die
In witness of Thy Unity;
From dying lips the accents swell,
"Thy God is One, O Israel;"
And bridegroom answers unto bride,
"The Lord is God, and none beside;"
And, knit with bonds of holiest faith,
They pass to endless life through death.

KALONYMOS BEN JEHUDA
Translation from the German by E. H. Plumptre

72

THE JEWS OF YORK

(From *Curiosities of Literature*)

Among the most interesting passages of history are those in which we contemplate an oppressed, yet sublime spirit, agitated by the conflict of two terrific passions: implacable hatred attempting a resolute vengeance, while that vengeance, though impotent, with dignified and silent horror, sinks into the last expression of despair. In a degenerate nation, we may, on such rare occasions, discover among them a spirit superior to its companions and its fortune.

In the ancient and modern history of the Jews we may find two kindred examples. I refer the reader for the more ancient narrative, to the second book of the Maccabees, chap. xiv. v. 37. No feeble and unaffecting painting is presented in the simplicity of the original. I proceed to relate the narrative of the Jews of York.

When Richard I ascended the throne, the Jews, to conciliate the royal protection, brought their tributes. Many had hastened from remote parts of England, and appearing at Westminster, the court and the mob imagined that they had leagued to bewitch his majesty. An edict was issued to forbid their presence at the coronation; but several, whose curiosity was greater than their prudence, conceived that they might pass unobserved among the crowd, and ventured to insinuate themselves into the abbey. Probably their voice and their visage alike betrayed them, for they were soon discovered; they flew diversely in great consternation, while many were dragged out with little remains of life.

A rumor spread rapidly through the city, that in honor of the festival, the Jews were to be massacred. The populace, at once eager of royalty and riot, pillaged and burnt their houses, and murdered the devoted Jews. Benedict, a Jew of York, to save his life, received baptism; and returning to that city, with his friend Jocenus, the most opulent of the Jews, died of his wounds. Jocenus and his servants narrated the late tragic circumstances to their neighbors, but where they hoped to move sympathy, they excited rage. The people at York soon gathered to imitate the people at London; and their first assault was on the house of the late Benedict, which having some strength and magnitude, contained his family and friends, who found their graves in its ruins. The alarmed Jews hastened to Jocenus, who conducted them to the governor of York Castle, and prevailed on him to afford them an asylum for their persons and effects. In the meanwhile their habitations were levelled, and the owners murdered, except a few unresisting beings, who, unmanly in sustaining honor, were adapted to receive baptism.

The castle had sufficient strength for their defence; but a suspicion arising that the governor, who often went out, intended to betray them, they one day refused him entrance. He complained to the sheriff of the county, and the chiefs of the violent party, who stood deeply indebted to the Jews, uniting with him, orders were issued to attack the castle. The cruel multitude, united with the soldiery, felt such a desire of slaughtering those they intended to despoil, that the sheriff, repenting of the order, revoked it, but in vain; fanaticism and robbery once set loose will satiate their appetency for blood and plunder. They solicited the aid of the superior citizens, who, perhaps not owing quite so much money to the Jews, humanely refused it; but having addressed the clergy (the barbarous clergy of those days), were by them animated, conducted, and blest.

The leader of this rabble was a canon regular, whose zeal was so fervent that he stood by them in his surplice, which he considered as a coat of mail, and reiteratedly exclaimed, "Destroy the enemies of Jesus!" This spiritual laconism invigorated the arm of men who perhaps wanted no other stimulative than the hope of obtaining the immense property of the besieged. It is related of this canon, that every morning before he went to assist in battering the walls, he swallowed a consecrated wafer. One day having approached too near, defended as he conceived by his surplice, this church militant was crushed by a heavy fragment of the wall, rolled from the battlement.

But the avidity of certain plunder prevailed over any reflection, which, on another occasion, the loss of so pious a leader might have raised. Their attacks continued; till at length the Jews perceived they could hold out no longer, and a council was called, to consider what remained to be done in the extremity of danger.

Among the Jews, their elder Rabbin was most respected. It has been customary with this people to invite for this place some foreigner, renowned among them for the depth of his learning, and the sanctity of his manners. At this time the *Haham*, or elder Rabbin, was a foreigner, who had been sent over to instruct them in their laws, and was a person, as we shall observe, of no ordinary qualifications.

When the Jewish council was assembled, the Haham rose, and addressed them in this manner: "Men of Israel! the God of our ancestors is omniscient, and there is no one who can say, Why doest thou this? This day he commands us to die for his law; for that law which we have cherished from the first hour it was given, which we have preserved pure throughout our captivity in all nations, and which for the many consolations it has given us, and the eternal hope it communicates, can we do less than die? Posterity shall behold this book of truth, sealed with our blood; and our death, while it displays our sincerity, shall impart confidence to the wanderer of Israel. Death is before our eyes; and we have only to choose an honorable and easy one. If we fall into the hands of our enemies, which you know we cannot escape, our death will be ignominious and cruel; for these Christians, who picture the spirit of God in a dove, and confide in the meek Jesus, are athirst for our blood, and prowl around the castle like wolves. It is therefore my advice that we elude their tortures; that we ourselves should be our own executioners; and that we voluntarily surrender our lives to our Creator. We trace the invisible Jehovah in his acts; God seems to call for us, but let us not be unworthy of that call. Suicide, on occasions like the present, is both rational and lawful; many examples are not wanting among our forefathers: as I advise, men of Israel, they have acted on similar occasions." Having said this, the old man sat down and wept.

The assembly was divided in their opinions. Men of fortitude applauded its wisdom, but the pusillanimous murmured that it was a dreadful counsel.

Again the Rabbin rose, and spoke these few words in a firm and decisive tone. "My children! since we are not unanimous in our opinions, let those who do not approve of my advice depart from this assembly!"—Some departed, but the greater number attached themselves to their venerable priest. They now employed themselves in consuming their valuables by fire; and every man, fearful of trusting to the timid and irresolute hand of the women, first destroyed his wife and children, and then himself. Jocenus and the Rabbin alone remained. Their life was protracted to the last, that they might see everything performed, according to their orders. Jocenus being the chief Jew was distinguished by the last mark of human respect in receiving his death from the consecrated hand of the aged Rabbin, who immediately after performed the melancholy duty on himself.

All this was transacted in the depth of the night. In the morning the walls of the castle were seen wrapt in flames, and only a few miserable and pusillanimous beings, unworthy of the sword, were viewed on the battlements, pointing to their extinct brethren. When they opened the gates of the castle, these men verified the prediction of their late Rabbin; for the multitude, bursting through the solitary courts, found themselves defrauded of their hopes, and in a moment avenged themselves on the feeble wretches, who knew not to die with honor.

Such is the narrative of the Jews of York, of whom the historian can only cursorily observe that five hundred destroyed themselves; but it is the philosopher who inquires into the causes and the manner of these glorious suicides. These are histories which meet only the eye of few, yet they are of infinitely more advantage than those which are read by everyone. We instruct ourselves in meditating on these scenes of heroic exertion; and if by such histories we make but a slow progress in chronology, our heart is, however, expanded with sentiment.

I admire not the stoicism of Cato, more than the fortitude of the Rabbin; or rather we should applaud that of the Rabbin much more; for Cato was familiar with the animating visions of Plato, and was the associate of Cicero and of Cæsar.

The Rabbin had probably read only the Pentateuch, and mingled with companions of mean occupations and meaner minds. Cato was accustomed to the grandeur of the mistress of the universe, and the Rabbin to the littleness of a provincial town. Men, like pictures, may be placed in an obscure and unfavorable light ; but the finest picture, in the unilluminated corner, still retains the design and coloring of the master. My Rabbin is a companion for Cato. His history is a tale
"Which Cato's self had not disdained to hear."—POPE

ISAAC DISRAELI

73

TRIAL OF REBECCA

(From *Ivanhoe*)

The ponderous castle-bell had tolled the point of noon, when Rebecca heard a trampling of feet upon the private stair which led to her place of confinement. . . . . . . The door of the chamber was unlocked, and Conrade and the Preceptor Malvoisin entered, attended by four warders clothed in black, and bearing halberds.

"Daughter of an accursed race !" said the Preceptor, " arise and follow us."

"Whither," said Rebecca, "and for what purpose ?"

"Damsel," answered Conrade, "it is not for thee to question, but to obey. Nevertheless, be it known to thee, that thou art to be brought before the tribunal of the Grand Master of Our Holy Order, there to answer for thine offences."

"May the God of Abraham be praised!" said Rebecca, folding her hands devoutly; "the name of a judge, though an enemy of my people, is to me the name of a protector. Most willingly do I follow thee—permit me only to wrap my veil around my head."

They descended the stair with slow and solemn step, traversed a long gallery, and, by a pair of folding doors placed at the end, entered the great hall in which the Grand Master had for the time established his court of justice.

The lower part of this ample apartment was filled with squires and yeomen, who made way not without some difficulty for Rebecca, attended by the Preceptor, and followed by the guard of halberdiers, to move forward to the seat appointed for her. As she passed through the crowd, a scrap of paper was thrust into her hand, which she received almost unconsciously, and continued to hold without examining its contents.

. . . .

The tribunal, erected for the trial of the innocent and unhappy Rebecca, occupied the dais or elevated part of the upper end of the great hall. . . . .

On an elevated seat, directly before the accused, sat the Grand Master of the Temple in full and ample robes of flowing white, holding in his hand the mystic staff, which bore the symbol of the Order. At his feet was placed a table, occupied by two scribes, chaplains of the Order, whose duty it was to reduce to formal record the proceedings of the day. The black dresses, bare scalps, and demure looks of these churchmen, formed a strong contrast to the warlike appearance of the knights who attended, either as residing in the Preceptory, or as come thither to attend upon their Grand Master.

. . . .

The remaining and lower part of the hall was filled with guards, holding partizans, and with other attendants whom curiosity had drawn thither, to see at once a Grand Master and a Jewish sorceress.

. . . .

A psalm . . . commenced the proceedings of the day; and the solemn sounds, *Venite exultemus Domino*, so often sung by the Templars before engaging with earthly adversaries, was judged by Lucas most appropriate to introduce the approaching triumph, for such he deemed it, over the powers of darkness.

. . . .

The Grand Master then raised his voice, and addressed the assembly.

"Reverend and valiant men, Knights, Preceptors, and Companions of this Holy Order, my brethren and my children!—you also, well-born and pious Esquires, who aspire to wear this Holy Cross!—and you also, Christian brethren, of every degree! —Be it known to you, that it is not defect of power in us which hath occasioned the assembling of this congregation; for, however unworthy in our person, yet to us is committed, with this batoon, full power

to judge and to try all that regards the weal of this our Holy Order. . . . . . But when the raging wolf hath made an inroad upon the flock, and carried off one member thereof, it is the duty of the kind shepherd to call his comrades together, that with bows and slings they may quell the invader. . . . . We have therefore summoned to our presence a Jewish woman, by name Rebecca, daughter of Isaac of York—a woman infamous for sortileges and for witcheries; whereby she hath maddened the blood, and besotted the brain, not of a churl, but of a Knight,—not of a secular Knight, but of one devoted to the service of the Holy Temple—not of a Knight Companion, but of a Preceptor of our Order, first in honor as in place.
. . . .
If we were told that such a man, so honored, and so honorable, suddenly casting away regard for his character, his vows, his brethren, and his prospects, had associated to himself a Jewish damsel, wandered in this company through solitary places, defended her person in preference to his own . . . . what should we say but that the noble Knight was possessed by some evil demon, or influenced by some wicked spell? . . . . If by means of charms and of spells, Satan had obtained dominion over the Knight . . . . we are then rather to lament than chastise his backsliding; and, imposing on him only such penance as may purify him from his iniquity, we are to turn the full edge of our indignation upon the accursed instrument, which had so well-nigh occasioned his utter falling away.

—Stand forth, therefore, and bear witness, ye who have witnessed these unhappy doings, that we may judge of the sum and bearing thereof; and judge whether our justice may be satisfied with the punishment of this infidel woman, or if we must go on, with a bleeding heart, to the further proceedings against our brother."

Several witnesses were called upon to prove the risks to which Bois-Guilbert exposed himself in endeavoring to save Rebecca from the burning castle, and his neglect of his personal defence in attending to her safety. The men gave these details with the exaggerations common to vulgar minds which have been strongly excited by any remarkable event, and their natural disposition to the marvellous was greatly increased by the satisfaction which their evidence seemed to afford to the eminent person for whose information it had been delivered.

. . . .

"Were it not well, brethren," said the Grand Master, "that we examine something into the former life and conversation of this woman, specially that we may discover whether she be one likely to use magical charms and spells, since the truths which we have heard may well incline us to suppose, that in this unhappy course our erring brother has been acted upon by some infernal enticement and delusion. . . . . Let those who have aught to witness of the life and conversation of this Jewish woman, stand forth before us." There was a bustle in the lower part of the hall, and when the Grand Master inquired the reason, it was replied, there was in the crowd a bedridden man, whom the prisoner had restored to the perfect use of his limbs by a miraculous balsam.

The poor peasant, a Saxon by birth, was dragged forward to the bar, terrified at the penal consequences which he might have incurred by the guilt of having been cured of the palsy by a Jewish damsel. Perfectly cured he certainly was not, for he supported himself forward on crutches to give evidence. Most unwilling was his testimony, and given with many tears; but he admitted that two years since, when residing at York, he was suddenly afflicted with a sore disease, while laboring for Isaac the rich Jew, in his vocation of a joiner: that he had been unable to stir from his bed until the remedies applied by Rebecca's directions, and especially a warming and spicy-smelling balsam, had in some degree restored him to the use of his limbs. Moreover, he said, she had given him a pot of that precious ointment, and furnished him with a piece of money withal, to return to the house of his father, near to Templestowe. "And may it please your gracious Reverence," said the man, "I cannot think the damsel meant harm by me, though she hath the ill hap to be a Jewess; for even when I used her remedy, I said the Pater and the Creed, and it never operated a whit less kindly."

"Peace, slave," said the Grand Master, "and begone! It well suits brutes like thee to be tampering with hellish cures, and to be giving your labor to the sons of mischief. I tell thee, the fiend can impose diseases for the very purpose of removing them, in order to bring into credit some diabolical fashion of cure. Hast thou that unguent of which thou speakest?"

The peasant, fumbling in his bosom with a trembling hand, produced a small box, bearing some Hebrew characters on the lid, which was, with most of the audience, a sure proof that the devil had stood apothecary. Beaumanoir, after crossing himself, took the box into his hand, and, learned in most of the Eastern tongues, read with ease the motto on the lid,—*The lion of the tribe of Judah has conquered.* "Strange powers of Sathanas," said he, "which can convert Scripture into blasphemy, mingling poison with our necessary food!—Is there no leech here who can tell us the ingredients of this mystic unguent?"

Two mediciners, as they called themselves, the one a monk, the other a barber, appeared, and avouched they knew nothing of the materials, excepting that they savored of myrrh and camphire, which they took to be Oriental herbs. But with the true professional hatred to a successful practitioner of their art, they insinuated that, since the medicine was beyond their own knowledge, it must necessarily have been compounded from an unlawful and magical pharmacopœia. . . When this medical research was ended, the Saxon peasant desired humbly to have back the medicine which he had found so salutary; but the Grand Master frowned severely at the request. "What is thy name, fellow?" said he to the cripple.

"Higg, the son of Snell," answered the peasant. "Then Higg, son of Snell," said the Grand Master, "I tell thee it is better to be bedridden, than to accept the benefit of unbelievers' medicine that thou mayest arise and walk; better to despoil infidels of their treasure by the strong hand, than to accept of them benevolent gifts, or do them service for wages. Go thou, and do as I have said."

"Alack," said the peasant, "an it shall not displease your Reverence, the lesson comes too late for me, for I am but a maimed man; but I will tell my two brethren, who serve the rich Rabbi, Nathan Ben Samuel, that your mastership says it is more lawful to rob him than to render him faithful service." . . . .

At this period of the trial, the Grand Master commanded Rebecca to unveil herself. Opening her lips for the first time, she replied patiently, but with dignity,—"that it was not the wont of the daughters of her people to uncover their faces when alone in an assembly of strangers." The sweet tones of her voice, and the softness of her reply, impressed on the audience a sentiment of pity and sympathy. But Beaumanoir, in whose mind the suppression of each feeling of humanity which could interfere with his imagined duty, was a virtue of itself, repeated his commands that his victim should be unveiled. The guards were about to remove her veil accordingly, when she stood up before the Grand Master and said, "Nay, but for the love of your own daughters—Alas!" she said, recollecting herself, "ye have no daughters!—yet for the remembrance of your mothers for the love of your sisters, and of female decency, let me not be thus handled in your presence; it suits not a maiden to be disrobed by such rude grooms. I will obey you," she added with an expression of patient sorrow in her voice, which had almost melted the heart of Beaumanoir himself; "ye are elders among your people, and at your command I will show the features of an ill-fated maiden."

She withdrew her veil and looked on them with a countenance in which bashfulness contended with dignity. Her exceeding beauty excited a murmur of surprise. . . . .

But Higg, the son of Snell, felt most deeply the effect produced by the sight of the countenance of his benefactress. "Let me go forth," he said to the warders at the door of the hall—"let me go forth!—To look at her again will kill me, for I have had a share in murdering her."

"Peace, poor man," said Rebecca, when she heard his exclamation; "thou hast done me no harm by speaking the truth—thou canst not aid me by thy complaints or lamentations. Peace, I pray thee—go home and save thyself." . . . .

The two men-at-arms, with whom Albert Malvoisin had not failed to communicate upon the import of their testimony, were now called forward. Though both were hardened and inflexible villains, the sight of the captive maiden, as well as her excelling beauty, at first appeared to stagger them; but an expressive glance from the Preceptor of

Templestowe restored them to their dogged composure, and they delivered, with a precision which would have seemed suspicious to more impartial judges, circumstances either altogether fictitious or trivial, and natural in themselves, but rendered pregnant with suspicion by the exaggerated manner in which they were told, and the sinister commentary which the witnesses added to the facts. The circumstances of their evidence would have been, in modern days, divided into two classes—those which were immaterial, and those which were actually and physically impossible.

. . . .

The Grand Master had collected the suffrages, and now in a solemn tone demanded of Rebecca what she had to say against the sentence of condemnation, which he was about to pronounce.

"To invoke your pity," said the lovely Jewess, with a voice somewhat tremulous with emotion, "would, I am aware, be as useless as I should hold it mean. To state that to relieve the sick and wounded of another religion, cannot be displeasing to the acknowledged Founder of both our faiths, were also unavailing; to plead that many things which these men (whom may Heaven pardon!) have spoken against me are impossible, would avail me but little, since you believe in their possibility; and still less would it advantage me to explain, that the peculiarities of my dress, language, and manners are those of my people—I had well-nigh said of my country, but alas! we have no country. Nor will I even vindicate myself at the expense of my oppressor, who stands there listening to the fictions and surmises which seem to convert the tyrant into the victim.- God be judge between him and me! . . . .

"But he is of your own faith, and his lightest affirmance would weigh down the most solemn protestations of the distressed Jewess. I will not therefore return to himself the charge brought against me—but to himself—yes, Brian de Bois-Guilbert, to thyself I appeal, whether these accusations are not false? as monstrous and calumnious as they are deadly?"

There was a pause; all eyes turned to Brian de Bois-Guilbert. He was silent.

"Speak," she said, "if thou art a man—a Christian, speak!—I conjure thee by the habit which thou dost wear, by the name thou dost inherit—by the knighthood thou dost vaunt—by the honor of thy mother—by the tomb and the bones of thy father—I conjure thee to say, are these things true?"

"Answer her, brother," said the Grand Master, "if the Enemy with whom thou dost wrestle will give thee power."

In fact, Bois-Guilbert seemed agitated by contending passions, which almost convulsed his features, and it was with a constrained voice that at last he replied, looking to Rebecca,—"The scroll! — the scroll!"

"Ay," said Beaumanoir, "this is indeed testimony! The victim of her witcheries can only name the fatal scroll, the spell inscribed on which is, doubtless, the cause of his silence."

But Rebecca put another interpretation on the words extorted as it were from Bois-Guilbert, and glancing her eye upon the slip of parchment which she continued to hold in her hand, she read written thereupon in the Arabian character, *Demand a champion!* The murmuring commentary which ran through the assembly at the strange reply of Bois-Guilbert gave Rebecca leisure to examine and instantly to destroy the scroll unobserved. When the whisper had ceased, the Grand Master spoke.

"Rebecca, thou canst derive no benefit from the evidence of this unhappy Knight, for whom, as we well perceive, the Enemy is yet too powerful. Hast thou aught else to say?"

"There is yet one chance of life left to me," said Rebecca, "even by your own fierce laws. Life has been miserable—miserable, at least, of late—but I will not cast away the gift of God, while he affords me the means of defending it. I deny this charge —I maintain my innocence, and I declare the falsehood of this accusation—I challenge the privilege of trial by combat, and will appear by my champion."

"And who, Rebecca," replied the Grand Master, "will lay lance in rest for a sorceress? who will be the champion of a Jewess?"

"God will raise me up a champion," said Rebecca —"It cannot be that in merry England—the hospitable, the generous, the free, where so many are ready to peril their lives for honor, there will not be found one to fight for justice. But it is enough that I challenge the trial by combat—there lies my gage."

She took her embroidered glove from her hand,
and flung it down before the Grand Master with an
air of mingled simplicity and dignity, which excited
universal surprise and admiration.

SIR WALTER SCOTT

74

THE JEW'S GIFT

A.D. 1200

The Abbot willed it, and it was done.
They hanged him high in an iron cage
For the spiteful wind and the patient sun
To bleach him. Faith, 't was a cruel age!
Just for no crime they hanged him there.
When one is a Jew, why, one remains
A Jew to the end, though he swing in air
From year to year in a suit of chains.

'Twas May, and the buds into blossom broke,
And the apple-boughs were pink and white:
What grewsome fruit was that on the oak,
Swaying and swaying, day and night!
The miller, urging his piebald mare
Over the cross-road, stopped and leered;
But never an urchin ventured there,
For fear of the dead man's long white beard.

A long white beard like carded wool,
Reaching down to the very knee—
Of the proper sort with which to pull
A heretic Jew to the gallows-tree!

Piteous women-folk turned away,
Having no heart for such a thing;
But the blackbirds on the alder-spray
For very joy of it seemed to sing.

Whenever a monk went shuffling by
To the convent over against the hill,
He would lift a pitiless pious eye,
And mutter, "The Abbot but did God's will!"
And the Abbot himself slept no whit less,
But rather the more, for this his deed :
And the May moon filled, and the loveliness
Of springtide flooded upland and mead.

Then an odd thing chanced. A certain clown,
On a certain morning breaking stone
By the hill-side, saw, as he glanced down,
That the heretic's long white beard was gone—
Shaved as clean and close as you choose,
As close and clean as his polished pate!
Like wild-fire spread the marvellous news,
From the ale-house bench to the convent gate.

And the good folk flocked from far and near,
And the monks trooped down the rocky height :
'Twas a miracle, that was very clear—
The Devil had shaved the Israelite!
Where is the Abbot? Quick, go tell!
Summon him, knave, God's death! straightway!
The Devil hath sent his barber from hell,
Perchance there will be the Devil to pay!

Now a lad that had climbed an alder-tree,
The better to overlook the rest,
Suddenly gave a shout of glee
At finding a wondrous blackbird-nest,
Then suddenly flung it from his hand,
For lo! it was woven of human hair,
Plaited and braided, strand upon strand —
No marvel the heretic's chin was bare!

Silence fell upon priest and clown,
Each stood riveted in his place ;
The brat that tugged at his mother's gown
Caught the terror that blanched her face.
Then one, a patriarch, bent and gray,
Wise with the grief of years fourscore,
Picked up his staff, and took his way
By the mountain-path to the Abbot's door—

And bravely told this thing of the nest,
How the birds had never touched cheek or eye,
But daintily plucked the fleece from the breast
To build a home for their young thereby.
"Surely, if they were not afeard
(God's little choristers, free of guile!)
To serve themselves of the Hebrew's beard,
It was that he was not wholly vile!

"Perhaps they saw with their keener eyes
The grace that we missed, but which God sees:
Ah, but He reads all hearts likewise,
The good in those, and the guilt in these.
Precious is mercy, O my lord!"
Humbly the Abbot bowed his head,

And making a gesture of accord—
"What would you have? The knave is dead."

"Certes, the man is dead! No doubt
Deserved to die; as a Jew, he died;
But now he hath served the sentence out
(With a dole or two thrown in beside),
Suffered all that he may of men—
Why not earth him, and no more words?"
The Abbot pondered, and smiled, and then—
"Well, well! since he gave his beard to the birds!"

THOMAS BAILEY ALDRICH

75

PLEA FOR THE JEWS BEFORE THE
COUNCIL AT NORDHAUSEN

(From *The Dance to Death*)

Tettenborn. Rabbi Jacob,
And thou, Süsskind von Orb, bow down, and learn
The Council's pleasure. You, the least despised
By true believers, and most reverenced
By your own tribe, we grace with our free leave
To enter, yea, to lift your voices here,
Amid these wise and honorable men,
If ye find aught to plead, that mitigates
The just severity of your doom. Our prince,
Frederick the Grave, Patron of Nordhausen,
Ordains that all the Jews within his lands,

For the foul crime of poisoning the wells,
Bringing the Black Death upon Christendom,
Shall be consumed with flame.
   Rabbi Jacob. I' the name of God,
Your God and ours, have mercy!
   Süsskind. Noble lords,
Burghers and artisans of Nordhausen,
Wise, honorable, just, God-fearing men,
Shall ye condemn or ever ye have heard?
Sure, one at least owns here the close, kind name
Of Brother—unto him I turn. At least,
Some sit among you who have wedded wives,
Bear the dear title and the precious charge
Of Husband—unto these I speak. Some here
Are crowned, it may be, with the sacred name
Of Father—unto these I pray. All, all
Are sons—all have been children, all have known
The love of parents—unto these I cry:
Have mercy on us, we are innocent,
Who are brothers, husbands, fathers, sons as ye!
Look you, we have dwelt among you many years,
Led thrifty, peaceable, well-ordered lives.
Who can attest, who prove we ever wrought
Or ever did devise the smallest harm,
Far less this fiendish crime against the State?
Rather let those arise who owe the Jews
Some debt of unpaid kindness, profuse alms,
The Hebrew leech's serviceable skill,
Who know our patience under injury,
And ye would see, if all stood bravely forth,
A motley host, led by the Landgrave's self,
Recruited from all ranks, and in the rear,

The humblest, veriest wretch in Nordhausen.
We know the Black Death is a scourge of God.
Is not our flesh as capable of pain,
Our blood as quick envenomed as your own?
Has the Destroying Angel passed the posts
Of Jewish doors- to visit Christian homes?
We all are slaves of one tremendous Hour.
We drink the waters that our enemies say
We spoil with poison,—we must breathe, as ye,
The universal air,—we droop, faint, sicken,
From the same causes to the selfsame end.
Ye are not strangers to me, though ye wear
Grim masks to-day—lords, knights, and citizens,
Few do I see whose hand has pressed not mine,
In cordial greeting. Dietrich von Tettenborn,
If at my death my wealth be confiscate
Unto the State, bethink you, lest she prove
A harsher creditor than I have been.
Stout Meister Rolapp, may you never again
Languish so nigh to death that Simon's art
Be needed to restore your lusty limbs.
Good Hugo Schultz—ah! be those blessed tears
Remembered unto you in Paradise!
Look there, my lords, one of your council weeps,
If you be men, why, then an angel sits
On yonder bench. You have good cause to weep,
You who are Christian, and disgraced in that
Whereof you made your boast. I have no tears.
A fiery wrath has scorched their source, a voice
Shrills through my brain—"Not upon us, on them
Fall everlasting woe, if this thing be!"

. . . .

Rabbi Jacob. Your pardon, lords,
I think you know not just what you would do.
You say the Jews shall burn—shall burn you say;
Why, good my lords, the Jews are not a flock
Of gallows-birds, they are a colony
Of kindly, virtuous folk. Come home with me;
I'll show you happy hearths, glad roofs, pure lives.
Why, some of them are little quick-eyed boys,
Some, pretty, ungrown maidens—children's children
Of those who called me to the pastorate.
And some are beautiful tall girls, some, youths
Of marvellous promise, some are old and sick,
Amongst them there be mothers, infants, brides,
Just like your Christian people, for all the world.
Know ye what burning is? Hath one of you
Scorched ever his soft flesh, or singed his beard,
His hair, his eyebrows—felt the keen, fierce nip
Of the pungent flame—and raises not his voice
To stop this holocaust? God! 'tis too horrible!
Wake me, my friends, from this terrific dream.
. . . .

Schnetzen. Enough! I pray you, my lord President,
End this unseemly scene. . . . .
. . . . Send the twain
Back to their people, that the court's decree
Be published unto all.
Süsskind. Lord Tettenborn!
Citizens! will you see this nameless crime
Brand the clean earth, blacken the crystal heaven?
Why, no man stirs! God! with what thick strange fumes

Hast thou, o' the sudden, brutalized their sense;
Or am I mad? Is this already hell?
Worshipful fiends, I have good store of gold,
Packed in my coffers, or loaned out to—Christians;
I give it you as free as night bestows
Her copious dews—my life shall seal the bond,
Have mercy on my race!
   Tettenborn.   No more, no more!
Go, bid your tribe make ready for their death
At sunset.

   .   .   .   .

   Süsskind.   Courage, brother,
Our fate is sealed. These tigers are athirst.
Return we to our people to proclaim
The gracious sentence of the noble court.
Let us go thank the Lord, who made us those
To suffer, not to do, this deed.

                                     EMMA LAZARUS

76
EXHORTATION TO THE JEWS OF NORDHAUSEN.

(From *The Dance to Death*)

Rabbi Jacob. The Lord is nigh unto the broken
   heart.
Out of the depths we cry to thee, oh God!
Show us the path of everlasting life;
For in thy presence is the plenitude
Of joy, and in thy right hand endless bliss.

Süsskind. Brethren, my cup is full!
Oh let us die as warriors of the Lord.
The Lord is great in Zion. Let our death
Bring no reproach to Jacob, no rebuke
To Israel. Hark ye! let us crave one boon
At our assassins' hands; beseech them build
Within God's acre where our fathers sleep,
A dancing-floor to hide the fagots stacked.
Then let the minstrels strike the harp and lute,
And we will dance and sing above the pile,
Fearless of death, until the flames engulf,
Even as David danced before the Lord,
As Miriam danced and sang beside the sea.
Great is our Lord. His name is glorious
In Judah, and extolled in Israel!
In Salem is his tent, his dwelling place
In Zion; let us chant the praise of God!
    A Jew. Süsskind, thou speakest well! we will
      meet death
With dance and song. Embrace him as a bride.
So that the Lord receive us in His tent.
    Several Voices. Amen! amen! amen! we dance
      to death.
    Rabbi Jacob. Süsskind, go forth and beg this
      grace of them.

. . . .

    Süsskind. Brethren, our prayer, being the last,
      is granted.
The hour approaches. Let our thoughts ascend
From mortal anguish, to the ecstasy
Of martyrdom, the blessed death of those
Who perish in the Lord. I see, I see

How Israel's ever-crescent glory makes
These flames that would eclipse it, dark as blots
Of candlelight against the blazing sun.
We die a thousand deaths,—drown, bleed, and burn ;
Our ashes are dispersed unto the winds.
Yet the wild winds cherish the sacred seed,
The waters guard it in their crystal heart,
The fire refuseth to consume. It springs,
A tree immortal, shadowing many lands,
Unvisited, unnamed, undreamed as yet.
Rather a vine full-flowered, golden-branched,
Ambrosial-fruited, creeping on the earth,
Trod by the passer's foot, yet chosen to deck
Tables of princes. Israel now has fallen
Into the depths, he shall be great in time.
Even as we die in honor, from our death
Shall bloom a myriad heroic lives,
Brave through our bright example, virtuous
Lest our great memory fall in disrepute.
Is one among us, brothers, would exchange
His doom against our tyrants,—lot for lot ?
Let him go forth and live—he is no Jew.
Is one who would not die in Israel
Rather than live in Christ,—their Christ who smiles
On such a deed as this ? Let him go forth—
He may die full of years upon his bed.
Ye who nurse rancor haply in your hearts,
Fear ye we perish unavenged ? not so !
To-day, no ! nor to-morrow ! but in God's time,
Our witnesses arise. Ours is truth,
Ours is the power, the gift of Heaven. We hold

His Law, His lamp, His covenant, His pledge.
Wherever in the ages shall arise
Jew-priest, Jew-poet, Jew-singer, or Jew-saint—
And everywhere I see them star the gloom—
In each of these the martyrs are avenged!
  Rabbi Jacob. Bring from the ark, the bell-
    fringed, silken-bound
Scrolls of the Law. Gather the silver vessels,
Dismantle the rich curtains of the doors,
Bring the perpetual lamp; all these shall burn,
For Israel's light is darkened, Israel's Law
Profaned by strangers. Thus the Lord has said:[1]
The weapon formed against thee shall not pros-
    per,
The tongue that shall contend with thee in judg-
    ment,
Thou shalt condemn. This is the heritage
Of the Lord's servants and their righteousness.
For thou shalt come to peoples yet unborn
Declaring that which He hath done. Amen.

EMMA LAZARUS

77

THE EXPULSION OF THE JEWS FROM SPAIN

(From *Coningsby*)

Whence came those Hebrew Arabs whose passage across the strait from Africa to Europe long

[1] Conclusion of service for Day of Atonement. E. L.

preceded the invasion of the Mohammedan Arabs, it is now impossible to ascertain. Their traditions tell us that from time immemorial they had sojourned in Africa; and it is not improbable that they may have been the descendants of some of the earlier dispersions; like those Hebrew colonies that we find in China, and who probably emigrated from Persia in the days of the great monarchies. Whatever may have been their origin in Africa, their fortunes in southern Europe are not difficult to trace, though the annals of no race in any age can detail a history of such strange vicissitudes, or one rife with more touching and romantic incident. Their unexampled prosperity in the Spanish Peninsula, and especially in the south, where they had become the principal cultivators of the soil, excited the jealousy of the Goths; and the Councils of Toledo during the sixth and seventh centuries attempted, by a series of decrees worthy of the barbarians who promulgated them, to root the Jewish Arabs out of the land. There is no doubt the Council of Toledo led as directly as the lust of Roderick to the invasion of Spain by the Moslemin Arabs. The Jewish population suffering under the most sanguinary and atrocious persecution looked to their sympathizing brethren of the Crescent, whose camps already gleamed on the opposite shore. The overthrow of the Gothic kingdoms was as much achieved by the superior information which the Saracens received from their suffering kinsmen, as by the resistless valor of the Desert. The Saracen kingdoms were established. That fair and unrivalled civilization arose, which preserved for Europe arts and letters when Christendom was plunged in darkness. The children of Ishmael rewarded the children of Israel with equal rights and privileges with themselves. During these halcyon centuries, it is difficult to distinguish the follower of Moses from the votary of Mahomet. Both alike built palaces, gardens, and fountains; filled equally the highest offices of the state, competed in an extensive and enlightened commerce, and rivalled each other in renowned universities.

Even after the fall of the principal Moorish kingdoms, the Jews of Spain were still treated by the conquering Goths with tenderness and consideration. Their numbers, their wealth, the fact that in Aragon especially, they were the proprietors of the soil, and surrounded by warlike and devoted followers, secured for them an usage which, for a considerable period, made them little sensible of the change of dynasties and religions. But the tempest gradually gathered. As the Goths grew stronger, persecution became more bold. Where the Jewish population was scanty, they were deprived of their privileges, or obliged to conform under the title of "Nuevos Christianos." At length the union of the two crowns under Ferdinand and Isabella, and the fall of the last Moorish kingdom, brought the crisis of their fate both to the New Christian and the non-conforming Hebrew. The Inquisition appeared—the institution that had exterminated the Albigenses and had desolated Languedoc, and which it should ever be remembered was established in the Spanish kingdoms against the protests of the Cortes and amid the terror of the populace. The Dominicans opened their first tribunal at Seville, and it is curious that the first individuals they summoned before them were the Duke of Medina Sidonia, the Marquess of Cadiz, and the Count of Arcos; three of the most considerable personages in Spain. How many were burned alive at Seville during the first year, how many imprisoned for life, what countless thousands were visited with severe though lighter punishments, need not be recorded here. In nothing was the Holy Office more happy than in multiform and subtle means by which they tested the sincerity of the New Christians.

At length the Inquisition was extended to Aragon. The high-spirited nobles of that kingdom knew that its institution was for them a matter of life or death. The Cortes of Aragon appealed to the King and to the Pope; they organized an extensive conspiracy; the chief Inquisitor was assassinated in the cathedral of Saragossa. Alas! it was fated that in this, one of the many and continual, and continuing struggles between the rival organizations of the North and the South, the children of the sun should fall. The fagot and the San Benito were the doom of the nobles of Aragon. Those who were convicted of secret Judaism, and this scarcely three centuries ago, were dragged to the stake; the sons of the noblest houses, in whose veins the Hebrew taint could be traced, had to walk in solemn procession, singing psalms, and confessing their faith in the religion of the fell Torquemada.

This triumph in Aragon, the almost simultaneous fall of the last Moorish kingdom, raised the hopes of the pure Christians to the highest pitch. Having purged the new Christians, they next turned their attention to the old Hebrews. Ferdinand was resolved that the delicious air of Spain should be breathed no longer by any one who did not profess the Catholic faith. Baptism or exile was the alternative. More than six hundred thousand individuals (some authorities greatly increase the amount), the most industrious, the most intelligent, and the most enlightened of Spanish subjects, would not desert the religion of their fathers. For this they gave up the delightful land wherein they had lived for centuries, the beautiful cities they had raised, the universities from which Christendom drew for ages its most precious lore, the tombs of their ancestors, the temples where they had worshipped the God for whom they made this sacrifice. They had but four months to prepare for eternal exile, after a residence of as many centuries; during which brief period forced sales and glutted markets virtually confiscated their property. It is a calamity that the scattered nation still ranks with the desolations of Nebuchadnezzar and of Titus. Who after this should say the Jews are by nature a sordid people? But the Spanish Goth, then so cruel and so haughty, where is he? A despised suppliant to the very race which he banished, for some miserable portion of the treasure which their habits of industry have again accumulated. Where is that tribunal that summoned Medina Sidonia and Cadiz to its dark inquisition? Where is Spain? Its fall, its unparalleled and its irremediable fall, is mainly to be attributed to the expulsion of that large portion of its subjects, the most industrious and intelligent, who traced their origin to the Mosaic and Mohammedan Arabs.

BENJAMIN DISRAELI

78

OF THE PROPHECIES CONCERNING THE DISPERSION AND RESTORATION OF THE JEWS

(From *Discourses on the Evidence of Revealed Religion*)

Moses, who so expressly foretold the dispersion of the Jews among the most distant nations of the world, says Lev. xxvi. 44, 45, "And yet for all that, when they shall be in the land of their enemies, I will not cast them away, neither will I abhor them, to destroy them utterly, and to break my covenant with them; for I am the Lord their God. But I will, for their sakes, remember the covenant of their ancestors, whom I brought forth out of the land of Egypt, in the sight of the Heathen, that I might be their God. I am the Lord."

Having foretold the dispersion of the Israelites into the most distant regions, he adds, Deut. iv.

29-31, "But if from thence thou shalt seek the Lord thy God, thou shalt find him, if thou seek him with all thy heart and with all thy soul. When thou art in tribulation, and all these things are come upon thee, even in the latter days, if thou turn to the Lord thy God, and shalt be obedient unto his voice (for the Lord thy God is a merciful God) he will not forsake thee, nor destroy thee, nor forget the covenant of thy fathers, which he sware unto them." . . . .

After Moses we find no prophecy relating to this subject till we come to the latter times of the kings of Judah, about eight hundred years before the Christian Era. But they abound in the writings of Joel, Amos, Hosea, Isaiah, Jeremiah, Ezekiel, Obadiah, and Daniel, before the return from Babylon, and in those of Haggai, Zechariah, and Malachi, after it. To quote the whole of what these prophets say on this subject, would be to copy a great part, if not the greater part, of their prophecies. For the future flourishing state of their nation is the great and favorite theme of all their writings. But as the subject is of particular importance, and appears to me not to have been sufficiently attended to, or understood, by Christians, who have supposed many of the prophecies to have been figurative, and to have been designed to express the state of the Christian Church, and not that of the Jewish nation, I shall recite a considerable number of the passages, to satisfy you they do not admit of any such figurative interpretation.

You will observe, as I recite them, that the prophecies concerning the restoration of the Israelites to the land of Palestine are generally accompanied with predictions of the glorious state of this extraordinary, though now despised and abject, nation, after their return, and also concerning the heavy judgments which will fall upon all the nations that have oppressed them, and especially those who shall oppose their return, or endeavor to disturb them after it. You will clearly see, from the express mention that is made of the quiet and undisturbed enjoyment of their country, which is promised to the Israelites, that these prophecies were by no means fulfilled at the return from the Babylonish captivity.

The predictions concerning the return of the ten tribes is a farther evidence of the same thing; besides that, after their restoration, all the twelve tribes are to make but one nation, and are to be governed by a prince of the house of David. Then also will be a time of universal peace and happiness through all the world, all mankind becoming worshippers of the one true God, and having the highest respect for his peculiar people, if not under some kind of subjection to them. I shall recite the passages according to the order of the time in which they were delivered, and without intermixing many particular observations by way of illustrations; for it will be seen that they require none.[1] . . . .

---

[1] The passages referred to, and omitted here, are Amos ix. 14, 15; Hosea iii. 4, 5; Isa. ii. 2-4; xi. 10-13; xliii. 5, 6; xlix.

With what feelings must pious Jews, in their present dispersed and oppressed state, meditate on such predictions as these that I have now read to you; and these, I may truly say, are not perhaps an hundredth part of what their prophets have delivered to them on this subject; for it is the great burden of all their writings. How must they be impressed with the idea of their nation being the chosen people of God, when they can trace their origin (which no other nation is able to do) from the first of the human race; when they can review all the wonderful dispensations of Providence respecting them; when they now find themselves in the very situation that Moses predicted more than three thousand years ago, and therefore can not entertain a doubt concerning the state of high pre-eminence over all other nations, which is with no less clearness promised to them in future time! Can we wonder at the firmness of the faith of the Jews, and at their adherence to their religion, when they are continually reading such prophecies as I have read to you? Can we wonder even at their pride, and undue contempt of all other nations? Who would not be proud of so illustrious a descent, and so glorious a destination as they alone can boast of? How little is the impression that the contempt of the world must have on such a people as this! To them it must be considered as the inso-

14-16, 22-26; liv. 5-8; lx. 4, 8-16; Zeph. iii. 19, 20; Jer. xvi. 14, 15; xxx. 3, 10, 11; Ezek. xxviii. 25; xxxvi. 24-28; xxxvii. 21, 22, 26-28; Zech. viii. 13-15, 20-23; xii. 9, 10; xiv. 11. 16-19; Mal. iii. 1-4, 12.

lence of beggars to princes in disguise. To correct
this pride, the most enlarged views, such as have
not yet opened to them, are necessary, viz., that
their God is as much the God and the Father of all
the human race as he is theirs, and that all pre-
eminence, under his government, has for its real
object, not the advantage of any part, though seem-
ingly the most favored, but of the whole of his
family; and therefore, though the Israelites will be
eminently distinguished and happy, it is only as the
means of blessing all the race of mankind, far more
numerous, and therefore, in the eye of God, far
more important than they.

. . . .

In the meantime, considering these very imper-
fect views of things, it becomes us to look princi-
pally to our own sentiments and conduct, and to be
careful to suppress within ourselves every affection
or sentiment that can, directly or indirectly, lead to
persecution, whether of Jews or Christians, and to
endeavor, as far as we can, to assist our persecuted
brethren, lightening the burdens that are imposed
by others.

JOSEPH PRIESTLEY

CIVIL DISABILITIES OF THE JEWS

(Extract from Speech in the House of Commons, April 5, 1830, on the "*Bill to Repeal the Civil Disabilities affecting British-born Subjects professing the Jewish Religion*")

In spite of the parallel which my honorable friend (the member for Oxford) has attempted—I think in vain—to draw between this case and the Roman Catholic measure before the House during the last Session of Parliament, I trust that we shall not have to forego the votes of many of those honorable gentlemen who in the last session were opposed to the concession of the Catholic claims. . . . . The general principle of religious toleration was involved in the question of last year, as it is now: but most of those gentlemen who voted against the Roman Catholics declared in favor of this general principle, only they found that there were special circumstances which took the case of the Roman Catholics out of the pale of that principle. But, Sir, there are no such circumstances here. In this instance, there is no foreign power to be feared. There is no divided allegiance threatening the State—there are no bulls—there are no indulgencies—there are no dispensations—there is no priesthood exercising an absolute authority over the consciences of those who are under their spiritual control—there are no agitators rousing and exciting the people to a course contrary to all good government—there are no associations assembling, or charged with assembling, for the purpose of assuming a power which ought only to belong to legally recognized functionaries—there are no mobs, disciplined to their task, and almost in the regular training of arms—there is no rent levied with the regularity of a tax. It was the fashion last year to declaim about a government that yielded to clamor, opposition, or threats, having betrayed the sacredness of its office, but there can be none such here; for even those most opposed to the present measure cannot deny that the Jews have borne their deprivations long in silence, and are now complaining with mildness and decency. . . The sect with which we now have to deal are even more prone to monopolize their religion than the others are to propagating the Catholic faith. Never has such a thing been heard of as an attempt on the part of the Jews to gain proselytes; and we may conclude, that with such rites and forms as belong to their faith, it could scarcely be expected by anyone that a scheme of proselytism could succeed with them. Be that, however, as it may, it is a thing at which they never appear to have aimed. On the contrary, they have always discouraged such an idea. Let the history of England be examined, and it will furnish topics enough against the Catholics. Those who have looked for such things have always found enough to talk about as to the crimes they have committed: the fires in Smithfield—the Gunpowder Plot—the Seven Bishops—have always afforded copious matter upon which to launch out in invective against the

Catholics. But with respect to the Jews, the history of England affords events exactly opposite; its pages, as to these people, are made up of wrongs suffered and injuries endured by them, without a trace of any wrong or injury committed in return; they are made up, from the beginning to the end, of atrocious cruelties inflicted on the one hand, and grievous privations endured for conscience sake on the other. . . . If this Bill, like the Roman Catholic one of last session, is to be opposed, it is condemning the strong and the weak, the violent and the patient, the proselyting and the exclusive, the political and the religious. If this is the course that is to be taken for our guide, persecution will never want an excuse, and the wolf will ever be able to invent a pretence to bear down and destroy the lamb. If this is to be the maxim set up for our landmark, it will soon appear that everything may be a reason with the aggressor, as everything is shown to be a crime in the aggressed. In all the opposition that was lately evinced against the Catholics, it was never once assumed or pretended that the opposition was religious; it was political and nothing else. . . . But now the whole case is changed. Political objection is fairly given up; and in its place religious persecution is avowed.

. . . .

All that the House has been told is, that the Jews are not Christians, and that therefore they must not have power. But this has not been declared openly and ingenuously, as it once was. Formerly the persecution of the Jews was at least consistent. The thing was made complete once by taking away their property, their liberty, and their lives. My honorable friend is now equally vehement about taking away their political power; and yet, no doubt, he would shudder at what such a measure would really take away. . . . If it was to be full and entire persecution, after the consistent example of our ancestors, I could understand it. If we were called on to revert to the days, when, as a people, they were pillaged—when their warehouses were torn down—when their every right was sacrificed, the thing would be comprehensible. But this is a delicate persecution, with no abstract rule for its guidance. As to the matter of right, if the word "legal" is to be attached to it, I am bound to acknowledge that the Jews have no legal right to power; but in the same way, 300 years ago, they had no legal right to be in England; and 600 years ago they had no legal right to the teeth in their heads: but if it is the moral right we are to look at, I say, that on every principle of moral obligation, I hold that the Jew has a right to political power. Every man has a right to all that may conduce to his pleasure, if it does not inflict pain on any one else. This is one of the broadest maxims of human nature, and I cannot therefore see how its supporters can be fairly called upon to defend it—the *onus probandi* lies, not on the advocates of freedom, but on the advocates of restraint. Let my honorable friend first show that there is some danger—some injury to the State, likely to arise from the admission of the Jews, and then will be the time to call upon us to answer the case that he has made out. Till such an argument, however, is fully made out, I shall contend for the moral right of the Jews. That they wish to have access to the privilege of sitting in Parliament has already been shown; it now remains to show that some harm is calculated to result from that admission. Unless this is shown, the refusal is neither more nor less than persecution. My honorable friend put a different interpretation upon the particular word I have used; but the meaning will still remain the same; and when we come to define the sense, it must be found, that we are only quibbling about a word. Any person may build a theory upon phrases: with some, perhaps, burning would be persecution, while the screwing of thumbs would not be persecution; others may call the screwing of thumbs persecution, and deny the justice of that expression when used to whipping. But according to my impression, the infliction of any penalties on account of religious opinions, and on account of religious opinions alone, is generally understood as coming within the meaning of the term, for all the purposes of political argument. It is as much persecution in principle as an *auto-da-fé*, the only difference is in degree. Defining persecution, then, as I do, I cannot conceive any argument to be adduced in favor of the mildest degree of this injustice, which, logically speaking, though not morally, indeed, might not be used with equal force in favor of the most cruel inflictions from similar motives. I have to make my apology for having occupied so much of the time of the honorable gentlemen present; but I could not refrain from making known my sentiments to this House of Commons, which has done more for the rights of conscience than any Parliament that ever sat. Its sessions of 1828 and 1829 have been marked by a glorious course in favor of religious liberty; and I hope that, before our separation, this Session of 1830 will put the finishing hand to that work which so many great and good men wish to see accomplished, but which cannot be, till this most desirable measure shall be carried into effect.

T. B. MACAULAY

80

CIVIL DISABILITIES OF THE JEWS

(Extract)

The distinguished member of the House of Commons who, towards the close of the last Parliament, brought forward a proposition for the relief of the Jews, has given notice of his intention to renew it. The force of reason in the last session carried the measure through one stage, in spite of the opposition of power. Reason and power are now on the same side; and we have little doubt that they will conjointly achieve a decisive victory. In order to contribute our share to the success of just principles, we propose to pass in review, as rapidly as possible, some of the arguments, or phrases claiming to be arguments, which have been employed to vindicate a system full of absurdity and injustice.

The Constitution, it is said, is essentially Christian; and, therefore, to admit Jews to office is to destroy the Constitution. Nor is the Jew injured by being excluded from political power. For no man has any right to power. A man has a right to his property; a man has a right to be protected from personal injury. These rights the law allows to the Jew; and with these rights it would be atrocious to interfere. But it is a mere matter of favor to admit any man to political power; and no man can justly complain that he is shut out from it.

We cannot but admire the ingenuity of this contrivance for shifting the burden of the proof from those to whom it properly belongs, and who would, we suspect, find it rather cumbersome. Surely no Christian can deny that every human being has a right to be allowed every gratification which produces no harm to others, and to be spared every mortification which produces no good to others. Is it not a source of mortification to a class of men that they are excluded from political power? If it be, they have, on Christian principles, a right to be freed from that mortification, unless it can be shown that their exclusion is necessary for the averting of some greater evil. The presumption is evidently in favor of toleration. It is for the prosecutor to make out his case.

The strange argument which we are considering would prove too much even for those who advance it. If no man has a right to political power, then neither Jew nor Gentile has such a right. The whole foundation of government is taken away.

But if government is taken away, the property
and the persons of men are insecure ; and it is acknowledged that men have a right to their property
and to personal security. . . . .

If there is any class of people who are not interested, or who do not think themselves interested,
in the security of property and the maintenance
of order, that class ought to have no share of the
powers which exist for the purpose of securing
property and maintaining order. But why a man
should be less fit to exercise those powers because
he wears a beard, because he does not eat ham,
because he goes to the synagogue on Saturdays
instead of going to the church on Sundays, we
cannot conceive.

The points of difference between Christianity
and Judaism have very much to do with a man's
fitness to be a bishop or a rabbi. But they have
no more to do with his fitness to be a magistrate,
a legislator, or a minister of finance, than with his
fitness to be a cobbler. Nobody has ever thought
of compelling cobblers to make any declaration on
the true faith of a Christian. Any man would
rather have his shoes mended by a heretical cobbler than by a person who had subscribed to all the
thirty-nine articles, but had never handled an awl.
Men act thus, not because they are indifferent to
religion, but because they do not see what religion
has to do with the mending of their shoes. Yet
religion has as much to do with the mending of
shoes as with the budget and the army estimates.
We have surely had several signal proofs within

the last twenty years that a very good Christian may be a very bad Chancellor of the Exchequer.

But it would be monstrous, say the persecutors, that Jews should legislate for a Christian community. This is a palpable misrepresentation. What is proposed is, not that the Jews should legislate for a Christian community, but that a legislature composed of Christians and Jews should legislate for a community composed of Christians and Jews. . . . .

That a Jew should be a judge in a Christian country would be most shocking. But he may be a juryman. He may try issues of fact ; and no harm is done. But if he should be suffered to try issues of law, there is an end of the Constitution. He may sit in a box plainly dressed, and return verdicts. But that he should sit on the bench in a black gown and white wig, and grant new trials, would be an abomination not to be thought of among baptized people. The distinction is certainly most philosophical. . . . .

That a Jew should be privy-councillor to a Christian king would be an eternal disgrace to the nation. But the Jew may govern the money-market, and the money-market may govern the world. The minister may be in doubt as to his scheme of finance till he has been closeted with the Jew. A congress of sovereigns may be forced to summon the Jew to their assistance. The scrawl of the Jew on the back of a piece of paper may be worth more than the royal word of three kings, or the national faith of three new American republics.

But that he should put Right Honorable before his name would be the most frightful of national calamities. . . . .

The English Jews, we are told, are not Englishmen. They are a separate people, living locally in this island, but living morally and politically in communion with their brethren who are scattered over all the world. An English Jew looks on a Dutch or a Portuguese Jew as his countryman, and on an English Christian as a stranger. This want of patriotic feeling, it is said, renders a Jew unfit to exercise political functions.

This argument has in it something plausible; but a close examination shows it to be quite unsound. Even if the alleged facts are admitted, still the Jews are not the only people who have preferred their sect to their country. The feeling of patriotism, when society is in a healthy state, springs up, by a natural and inevitable association, in the minds of citizens who know that they owe all their comforts and pleasures to the bond which unites them in one community. But, under a partial and oppressive government, these associations cannot acquire that strength which they have in a better state of things. Men are compelled to seek from their party that protection which they ought to receive from their country, and they, by a natural consequence, transfer to their party that affection which they would otherwise have felt for their country. The Huguenots of France called in the help of England against their Catholic kings. The Catholics of France called in the help of Spain against a Huguenot king. Would it be fair to infer, that at present the French Protestants would wish to see their religion made dominant by the help of a Prussian or English army? Surely not. And why is it that they are not willing, as they formerly were willing, to sacrifice the interests of their country to the interests of their religious persuasion? The reason is obvious: they were persecuted then, and are not persecuted now. The English Puritans, under Charles the First, prevailed on the Scotch to invade England. Do the Protestant Dissenters of our time wish to see the Church put down by an invasion of foreign Calvinists? If not, to what cause are we to attribute the change? Surely to this, that the Protestant Dissenters are far better treated now than in the seventeenth century.

Some of the most illustrious public men that England ever produced were inclined to take refuge from the tyranny of Laud in North America. Was this because Presbyterians and Independents are incapable of loving their country? But it is idle to multiply instances. Nothing is so offensive to a man who knows anything of history or of human nature as to hear those who exercise the powers of government accuse any sect of foreign attachments. If there be any proposition universally true in politics it is this, that foreign attachments are the fruit of domestic misrule.

. . . .

Rulers must not thus be suffered to absolve themselves of their solemn responsibility. It does not lie in their mouths to say that a sect is not patriotic. It is their business to make it patriotic. History and reason clearly indicate the means. The English Jews are, as far as we can see, precisely what our government has made them. They are precisely what any sect, what any class of men, treated as they have been treated, would have been. If all the red-haired people in Europe had, during centuries, been outraged and oppressed, banished from this place, imprisoned in that, deprived of their money, deprived of their teeth, convicted of the most improbable crimes on the feeblest evidence, dragged at horses' tails, hanged, tortured, burned alive, if, when manners became milder, they had still been subject to debasing restrictions and exposed to vulgar insults, locked up in particular streets in some countries, pelted and ducked by the rabble in others, excluded everywhere from magistracies and honors, what would be the patriotism of gentlemen with red hair? And if, under such circumstances, a proposition were made for admitting red-haired men to office, how striking a speech might an eloquent admirer of our old institutions deliver against so revolutionary a measure! "These men," he might say, "scarcely consider themselves as Englishmen. They think a red-haired Frenchman or a red-haired German more closely connected with them than a man with brown hair born in their own parish. If a foreign sovereign patronizes red hair, they love him better than their own native king. They are not Englishmen; they cannot be Englishmen; nature has forbidden it, experience proves it to be impossible. Right to political power they have none; for no man has a right to political power. Let them enjoy personal security, let their property be under the protection of the law. But if they ask for leave to exercise power over a community of which they are only half members—a community the constitution of which is essentially dark-haired—let us answer them in the words of our wise ancestors, *Nolumus leges Angliæ mutari."*

. . . .

There is another argument which we would not willingly treat with levity, and which yet we scarcely know how to treat seriously. Scripture, it is said, is full of terrible denunciations against the Jews. It is foretold that they are to be wanderers. Is it then right to give them a home? It is foretold that they are to be oppressed. Can we with propriety suffer them to be rulers? To admit them to the rights of citizens is manifestly to insult the Divine oracles.

We allow that to falsify a prophecy inspired by Divine Wisdom would be a most atrocious crime. It is, therefore, a happy circumstance for our frail species, that it is a crime which no man can possibly commit. If we admit the Jews to seats in Parliament, we shall, by so doing, prove that the prophecies in question, whatever they may mean, do not mean that the Jews shall be excluded from Parliament.

. . . .

T. B. MACAULAY

THE CROWING OF THE RED COCK

(1881)

Across the Eastern sky has glowed
    The flicker of a blood-red dawn,
Once more the clarion cock has crowed,
    Once more the sword of Christ is drawn.
A million burning rooftrees light
The world-wide path of Israel's flight.

Where is the Hebrew's fatherland?
    The folk of Christ is sore bestead;
The Son of Man is bruised and banned,
    Nor finds whereon to rest his head.
His cup is gall, his meat is tears,
His passion lasts a thousand years.

Each crime that wakes in man the beast,
    Is visited upon his kind.
The lust of mobs, the greed of priest,
    The tyranny of kings, combined
To root his seed from earth again,
His record is one cry of pain.

When the long roll of Christian guilt
    Against his sires and kin is known,
The flood of tears, the life-blood spilt,
    The agony of ages shown,
What oceans can the stain remove,
From Christian law and Christian love?

Nay, close the book; not now, not here,
    The hideous tale of sin narrate,
Reëchoing in the martyr's ear,
    Even he might nurse revengeful hate,
Even he might turn in wrath sublime,
With blood for blood and crime for crime.

Coward? Not he, who faces death,
    Who singly against worlds has fought,
For what? A name he may not breathe,
    For liberty of prayer and thought.
The angry sword he will not whet,
His nobler task is—to forget.

EMMA LAZARUS

82

THE BANNER OF THE JEW

Wake, Israel, wake! Recall to-day
    The glorious Maccabean rage,
The sire heroic, hoary-gray,
    His five-fold lion-lineage:
The Wise, the Elect, the Help-of-God,
The Burst-of-Spring, the Avenging-Rod.[1]

From Mizpeh's mountain-ridge they saw
    Jerusalem's empty streets, her shrine
Laid waste where Greeks profaned the Law,
    With idol and with pagan sign.
Mourners in tattered black were there,
With ashes sprinkled on their hair.

---

[1] The sons of Mattathias—Jonathan, John, Eleazar, Simon (also called the Jewel), and Judas, the Prince.

THE BANNER OF THE JEW

Then from the stony peak there rang
   A blast to ope the graves : down poured
The Maccabean clan, who sang
   Their battle-anthem to the Lord.
Five heroes lead, and following, see,
Ten thousand rush to victory.

Oh for Jerusalem's trumpet now,
   To blow a blast of shattering power,
To wake the sleepers high and low,
   And rouse them to the urgent hour!
No hand for vengeance—but to save,
A million naked swords should wave.

Oh deem not dead that martial fire,
   Say not the mystic flame is spent!
With Moses' Law and David's lyre,
   Your ancient strength remains unbent.
Let but an Ezra rise anew,
To lift the *Banner of the Jew!*

A rag, a mock at first—ere long,
   When men have bled and women wept,
To guard its precious folds from wrong,
   Even they who shrunk, even they who slept,
Shall leap to bless it, and to save.
Strike! for the brave revere the brave.

EMMA LAZARUS

THE LEGEND OF RABBI BEN LEVI

(From *Tales of a Wayside Inn*)

Rabbi Ben Levi, on the Sabbath, read
A volume of the Law, in which it said,
"No man shall look upon my face and live."
And as he read, he prayed that God would give
His faithful servant grace with mortal eye
To look upon His face and yet not die.

Then fell a sudden shadow on the page,
And, lifting up his eyes, grown dim with age,
He saw the Angel of Death before him stand,
Holding a naked sword in his right hand.
Rabbi Ben Levi was a righteous man,
Yet through his veins a chill of terror ran.
With trembling voice he said, "What wilt thou
 here?"
The Angel answered, "Lo! the time draws near
When thou must die; yet first, by God's decree,
Whate'er thou askest shall be granted thee."
Replied the Rabbi, "Let these living eyes
First look upon my place in Paradise."

Then said the Angel, "Come with me and look."
Rabbi Ben Levi closed the sacred book,
And rising, and uplifting his gray head,
"Give me thy sword," he to the Angel said,
"Lest thou shouldst fall upon me by the way."
The angel smiled and hastened to obey,

Then led him forth to the Celestial Town,
And set him on the wall, whence, gazing down,
Rabbi Ben Levi, with his living eyes,
Might look upon his place in Paradise.

Then straight into the city of the Lord
The Rabbi leaped with the Death-Angel's sword,
And through the streets there swept a sudden breath
Of something there unknown, which men call death.
Meanwhile the Angel stayed without, and cried,
" Come back ! " To which the Rabbi's voice replied,
" No ! in the name of God, whom I adore,
I swear that hence I will depart no more ! "

Then all the Angels cried, " O Holy One,
See what the son of Levi here hath done !
The kingdom of Heaven he takes by violence,
And in thy name refuses to go hence ! "
The Lord replied, " My Angels be not wroth;
Did e'er the son of Levi break his oath ?
Let him remain ; for he with mortal eye
Shall look upon my face and yet not die."

Beyond the outer wall the Angel of Death
Heard the great voice, and said, with panting breath,
"Give back the sword, and let me go my way."
Whereat the Rabbi paused, and answered, " Nay !
Anguish enough already hath it caused
Among the sons of men." And while he paused

He heard the awful mandate of the Lord
Resounding through the air, "Give back the sword!"

The Rabbi bowed his head in silent prayer;
Then said he to the dreadful Angel, "Swear,
No human eye shall look on it again;
But when thou takest away the souls of men,
Thyself unseen, and with an unseen sword,
Thou wilt perform the bidding of the Lord."
The Angel took the sword again, and swore,
And walks on earth unseen forevermore.

H. W. LONGFELLOW

84

SANDALPHON

Have you read in the Talmud of old,
In the Legends the Rabbins have told,
   Of the limitless realms of the air,
Have you read it,—the marvellous story
Of Sandalphon, the Angel of Glory,
   Sandalphon, the Angel of Prayer?

How, erect, at the outermost gates
Of the City Celestial he waits,
   With his feet on the ladder of light,
That, crowded with angels unnumbered,
By Jacob was seen, as he slumbered
   Alone in the desert at night?

The Angels of Wind and of Fire
Chant only one hymn, and expire
    With the song's irresistible stress;
Expire in their rapture and wonder,
As harp-strings are broken asunder
    By music they throb to express.

But serene in the rapturous throng,
Unmoved by the rush of the song,
    With eyes unimpassioned and slow,
Among the dead angels, the deathless
Sandalphon stands listening breathless
    To sounds that ascend from below;—

From the spirits on earth that adore,
From the souls that entreat and implore
    In the fervor and passion of prayer;
From the hearts that are broken with losses,
And weary with dragging the crosses
    Too heavy for mortals to bear.

And he gathers the prayers as he stands,
And they change into flowers in his hands,
    Into garlands of purple and red;
And beneath the great arch of the portal,
Through the streets of the City Immortal
    Is wafted the fragrance they shed.

It is but a legend, I know,—
A fable, a phantom, a show,
    Of the ancient Rabbinical lore;
Yet the old mediæval tradition,
The beautiful, strange superstition,
    But haunts me and holds me the more.

When I look from my window at night,
And the welkin above is all white,
　　All throbbing and panting with stars,
Among them majestic is standing
Sandalphon the angel, expanding
　　His pinions in nebulous bars.

And the legend, I feel, is a part
Of the hunger and thirst of the heart,
　　The frenzy and fire of the brain,
That grasps at the fruitage forbidden,
The golden pomegranates of Eden,
　　To quiet its fever and pain.

H. W. LONGFELLOW

85

THE RABBI'S VISION

Ben Levi sat with his books alone
　　At the midnight's solemn chime,
And the full-orb'd moon through his lattice shone
　　In the power of autumn's prime;
It shone on the darkly learned page,
And the snowy locks of the lonely Sage—
But he sat and mark'd not its silvery light,
For his thoughts were on other themes that night.

Wide was the learn'd Ben Levi's fame
　　As the wanderings of his race—
And many a seeker of wisdom came
　　To his lonely dwelling-place;
For he made the darkest symbols clear,
Of ancient doctor and early seer.

Yet a question ask'd by a simple maid
He met that eve in the linden's shade,
Had puzzled his matchless wisdom more
Than all that ever it found before;
And this it was—"What path of crime
Is darkliest traced on the map of time?"

The Rabbi ponder'd the question o'er
   With a calm and thoughtful mind,
And search'd the depths of the Talmud's lore—
   But an answer he could not find;—
Yet a maiden's question might not foil
A Sage inured to Wisdom's toil—
And he leant on his hand his aged brow,
For the current of thought ran deeper now:

When, lo! by his side, Ben Levi heard
   A sound of rustling leaves—
But not like those of the forest stirr'd
   By the breath of summer eves,
That comes through the dim and dewy shades
As the golden glow of the sunset fades,
Bringing the odors of hidden flowers
That bloom in the greenwood's secret bowers—

But the leaves of a luckless volume turn'd
   By the swift impatient hand
Of student young, or of critic learn'd
   In the lore of the Muse's land.
The Rabbi raised his wondering eyes—
Well might he gaze in mute surprise—
For, open'd wide to the moon's cold ray,
A ponderous volume before him lay!

Old were the characters, and black
As the soil when sear'd by the lightning's track,
But broad and full that the dimmest sight
Might clearly read by the moon's pale light ;
But, oh ! 'twas a dark and fearful theme
    That fill'd each crowded page—
The gather'd records of human crime
    From every race and age.

All the blood that the Earth had seen
Since Abel's crimson'd her early green ;
All the vice that had poison'd life
Since Lamech wedded his second wife ;
All the pride that had mock'd the skies
    Since they built old Babel's wall ;—
But the page of the broken promises
    Was the saddest page of all.

It seem'd a fearful mirror made
For friendship ruin'd and love betray'd,
For toil that had lost its fruitless pain,
And hope that had spent its strength in vain ;
For all who sorrow'd o'er broken faith—
Whate'er their fortunes in life or death—
Were there in one ghastly pageant blent
With the broken reeds on which they leant.

And foul was many a noble crest
    By the Nations deem'd unstain'd—
And, deep on brows which the Church had bless'd,
    The traitor's brand remain'd.

For vows in that blacken'd page had place
   Which Time had ne'er reveal'd,
And many a faded and furrow'd face
   By death and dust conceal'd—
Eyes that had worn their light away
In weary watching from day to day,
And tuneful voices which Time had heard
Grow faint with the sickness of hope deferr'd.

The Rabbi read till his eye grew dim
   With the mist of gathering tears,
For it woke in his soul the frozen stream
   Which had slumber'd there for years;
And he turn'd, to clear his clouded sight,
From that blacken'd page to the sky so bright—
And joy'd that the folly, crime, and care
Of Earth could not cast one shadow there.

For the stars had still the same bright look
   That in Eden's youth they wore;—
And he turn'd again to the ponderous book—
   But the book he found no more;
Nothing was there but the moon's pale beam—
And whence that volume of wonder came,
Or how it pass'd from his troubled view,
The Sage might marvel, but never knew!

Long and well had Ben Levi preach'd
   Against the sins of men—
And many a sinner his sermons reach'd,
   By the power of page and pen:
Childhood's folly, and manhood's vice,
And age with its boundless avarice,

All were rebuk'd, and little ruth
Had he for the venial sins of youth.

But never again to mortal ears
    Did the Rabbi preach of aught
But the mystery of trust and tears
    By that wondrous volume taught.
And if he met a youth and maid
    Beneath the linden boughs—
Oh, never a word Ben Levi said,
    But—"Beware of Broken Vows!"

FRANCES BROWNE

86

THE TWO RABBINS

The Rabbin Nathan twoscore years and ten
Walked blameless through the evil world, and then,
Just as the almond blossomed in his hair,
Met a temptation all too strong to bear,
And miserably sinned. So, adding not
Falsehood to guilt, he left his seat, and taught
No more among the elders, but went out
From the great congregation girt about
With sackcloth, and with ashes on his head,
Making his gray locks grayer. Long he prayed,
Smiting his breast; then, as the Book he laid
Open before him for the Bath-Col's choice,
Pausing to hear that Daughter of a Voice,
Behold the royal preacher's words: "A friend
Loveth at all times, yea, unto the end;

And for the evil day thy brother lives."
Marvelling, he said : " It is the Lord who gives
Counsel in need. At Ecbatana dwells
Rabbi Ben Isaac, who all men excels
In righteousness and wisdom, as the trees
Of Lebanon the small weeds that the bees
Bow with their weight. I will arise, and lay
My sins before him."
          And he went his way
Barefooted, fasting long, with many prayers ;
But even as one who, followed unawares,
Suddenly in the darkness feels a hand
Thrill with its touch his own, and his cheek
    fanned
By odors subtly sweet, and whispers near
Of words he loathes, yet cannot choose but hear,
So, while the Rabbi journeyed, chanting low
The wail of David's penitential woe,
Before him still the old temptation came,
And mocked him with the motion and the shame
Of such desires that, shuddering, he abhorred
Himself ; and, crying mightily to the Lord
To free his soul and cast the demon out,
Smote with his staff the blackness round about.

At length, in the low light of a spent day,
The towers of Ecbatana far away
Rose on the desert's rim ; and Nathan, faint
And footsore, pausing where for some dead saint
The faith of Islam reared a doměd tomb,
Saw some one kneeling in the shadow, whom

He greeted kindly: " May the Holy One
Answer thy prayers, O stranger!" whereupon
The shape stood up with a loud cry, and then,
Clasped in each other's arms, the two gray men
Wept, praising Him whose gracious providence
Made their paths one. But straightway, as the sense
Of his transgression smote him, Nathan tore
Himself away: "O friend beloved, no more
Worthy am I to touch thee, for I came,
Foul from my sins, to tell thee all my shame.
Haply thy prayers, since naught availeth mine,
May purge my soul, and make it white like thine.
Pity me, O Ben Isaac, I have sinned!"

Awestruck Ben Isaac stood. The desert wind
Blew his long mantle backward, laying bare
The mournful secret of his shirt of hair.
"I too, O friend, if not in act," he said,
"In thought have verily sinned. Hast thou not read,
'Better the eye should see than that desire
Should wander?' Burning with a hidden fire
That tears and prayers quench not, I come to thee
For pity and for help, as thou to me.
Pray for me, O my friend!" But Nathan cried,
"Pray thou for me, Ben Isaac!"

                              Side by side
In the low sunshine by the turban stone
They knelt; each made his brother's woe his own,
Forgetting, in the agony and stress
Of pitying love, his claim of selfishness;

Peace, for his friend besought, his own became;
His prayers were answered in another's name;
And, when at last they rose up to embrace,
Each saw God's pardon in his brother's face!

Long after, when his headstone gathered moss,
Traced on the targum-marge of Onkelos
In Rabbi Nathan's hand these words were read:
"*Hope not the cure of sin till Self is dead;
Forget it in love's service, and the debt
Thou canst not pay the angels shall forget;
Heaven's gate is shut to him who comes alone;
Save thou a soul, and it shall save thy own.*"

JOHN GREENLEAF WHITTIER

87

A LEGEND OF PARADISE

(From *The Son of a Star*)

I

O mighty Cherubin, with flaming sword
Before the gate! Before, before the gate!
   Touchless with human hands,
   Sightless with human eyes,
Portal of sinful mortal fate,
   The gate of Paradise!
Oh mighty Cherubin, speak but the word!
That I may see the garden of the Lord
   And grow more wise.

Thus spake the First of four of men who were
The living pillars of the deathless race.
Ezra! the scholar and the interpreter
Of the great book of life which time shall ne'er
    efface.

    Then from the flaming sword
    Came forth the sacred word,
    Enter thou faithful one;
    Thy work hath been well done,
    Enter the garden of the Lord.

    Beyond the sword of fire,
    Untouched by fire or sword,
    He gains his soul's desire,
    The garden of the Lord.

    That he may grow more wise
    He enters Paradise.
    Enters! Beholds! and Dies!

II

Oh dreaded Cherubin, whose flaming sword
Doth hide from mortal eyes the stream of life!
The tree of good and evil and its fruit;
The place where God breathed into man his breath;
The place where God and man spake word to word;
Where every living plant and herb and brute,
Was given man; and from him torn the wife
Whom the foul serpent led aside to death.
Oh dreaded Cherubin! grant my desire

Unquenchable as thy consuming fire,
Which guardeth Paradise!
That I may see the garden of the Lord
And grow more wise.

Thus spake the Second one who reached the goal.
Asaph ; a mystic form who shone,
As if his eager soul
Incarnate, would be gone ;
Leaving its fleshly dress
In this world's wilderness.

Straight from the lambent flame the words were
    said ;
If that thou fearest not to see
What made a brother scholar like to thee
Fall with the dead ;
Killed by the glory he could not survive.
    Then, true and faithful one!
    Whose work hath been well done,
Enter the garden of the Lord, and live.

Beyond the sword of fire,
Untouched by fire or sword,
He gains his soul's desire,
The garden of the Lord.

That he may grow more wise
He enters Paradise.
Enters! beholds from whence
They were expell'd who did at first transgress.
Enters, beholds and flies
Back to the wilderness,
Bereft of every sense!

III

Lo! glorious Cherubin with flaming sword!
Lo! I Elisha Ben Abuyah stand—
Stored with all learning gained in every land—
Before the gate whence Eve and Adam fled;
Asking of thee that I may freely tread
    The plains of Paradise.
That I may see the garden of the Lord
    And grow more wise.

Thus spake the Third in tones of majesty;
Elisha Ben Abuyah, who would pierce
The solid earth, the sea, the eternal space.
Not suppliant, but as a Deity,
Asking from God of God! as face to face
A ravenous man, feeling his hunger fierce,
Asks men to feed him to satiety.

Again the voice from out the flaming sword.
Thou son of subtlety and earthly pride!
Wherefore within thy mantle's flowing folds
Dost thou those books of Baal worship hide?
Our God, a jealous God, forever holds
Him lost to him who serveth him in part,
Giving the lip, yet keeping back the heart.

Elisha Ben Abuyah stood dismayed,
But gathering up his strength and bending low
Thus to the flaming Cherubin he said:
These treasured books, dear as my own heart's
    blood,
I burn! I burn! I burn! that I may know

The greater secret that before me lies,
The garden of the Lord saved from the flood,
The golden Paradise.

The flaming fire rose up and filled the skies:
  A burning sacrifice
Of all Elisha Ben Abuyah loved.
It is enough, the Cherubin replies,
Thou art forgiven, is the gracious word.
And, every barrier to thy wish removed,
  Enter the garden of the Lord.

  Beyond the sword of fire,
  Untouched by fire or sword,
  He gains his soul's desire,
  The garden of the Lord.

That he may grow more wise
He enters Paradise.
Boldly he looks around,
And treads the holy ground
As one who would declare,
I am the son and heir
Of him to whom these treasures all belong.
Rivers of life combine,
With the fruit of the Tree divine,
To nourish with marvels my tongue.
Of all that is here, as mine,
I will sing! I will write! I will tell!
From the gates of heaven to hell:
In parable, legend and song.

Filled with the curse of pride
Elisha Ben Abuyah makes his way,
Crushing with reckless stride
Whate'er before him lay.
Crushing the tender plants so young and sweet,
The plants of Paradise, beneath his feet.
What voice is that he hears,
That breaketh him with fears?
What pang is that he feels?
It is the voice of God,
The angel's flashing rod.
Oh thou who kills the plants of Paradise
That thou, vain man, may grow more wise!
Fly from my wrath back to the wilderness,
And seek again thine everlasting peace.
A lightning glance! a split of earth! a grave!
    Outside the flaming gate.
Elisha Ben Abuyah, who shall save
    Thee from thy fate?
In flight he falls into that open grave,
And as the flint upon the steel
Strikes into fire, so he upon the ground
Bursts into lurid flames, which he can feel
Yet never can extinguish. Years roll round;
Ages of sons of men sink down and die.
    Elisha Ben Abuyah to be wise
Killed the young plants of Paradise.
His light is wisdom's fool. He burns, but never
    dies.

IV

Oh faithful Cherubin, whose flaming sword
Doth hide the garden of the Holy One!
May I, a shepherd born in Israel's fold,
Ask thee to ask of him I dare not name,
Th' Omnipotent! World without end the same!
That I the last of those who stood alone
Interpreters of his most sacred word,
May through thy glory enter Paradise,
And by thy radiant wisdom grow more wise?

So spake the last of those who stood alone,
The matchless scholars of the deathless race.
Calm dignity from off his image shone,
Sweet modesty was written on his face,
With courage intermixed and gentle grace,
    All set in comeliness.

With cheerful voice the guardian spirit spoke:
Akiba the beloved, thy deeds are known.
He whom thou servest through thy nights and days
Hath read thy heart of hearts and seen thy ways.
Thou art to him a plain and open book,
And what thou askest now is all thine own;
Thine own for knowledge, wisdom, precept, word,
    Enter thou to the garden of the Lord.

    Beyond the sword of fire,
    Untouched by fire or sword,
    He gains his soul's desire,
    The garden of the Lord!

That he may grow more wise
Akiba enters Paradise.
His feet retrace each round
Of the enchanted ground,
Saved only of all gardens from the flood.
The tree of knowledge yields him living food.
Within the bower where Adam slept he sleeps
Fearing no evil: knowing well that He,
    Of omnipresent majesty!
The Holy One of Israel! keeps
His steps from falling and his sleep from fear,
Life of his life: unseen yet ever near.

That he might grow more wise,
Akiba entered Paradise,
Entered and lived and learned.
And when his wondrous task was done,
Back through the wilderness returned
To teach to every chosen son
Of Israel born, the sacred mysteries.

            BENJAMIN WARD RICHARDSON

88

THE DYING HEBREW'S PRAYER

(From *The Devil's Progress*)

A Hebrew knelt, in the dying light,—
His eye was dim and cold,
The hairs on his brow were silver-white,
And his blood was thin and old.

He lifted his look to his latest sun,
For he knew that his pilgrimage was done,
And as he saw God's *shadow* there,
His spirit poured itself in prayer.

" I come unto death's second-birth,
Beneath a stranger-air,
A pilgrim on a dull, cold earth,
As all my fathers were.
And men have stamped me with a curse,—
I feel it is not *Thine*,
Thy mercy—like yon sun—was made
On me—as them—to shine ;
And, therefore, dare I lift mine eye,
Through that, to Thee,—before I die !

" In this great temple, built by Thee,
Whose altars *are* divine,
Beneath yon lamp, that ceaselessly
Lights up Thine own true shrine,
O take my latest sacrifice,—
Look down, and make this sod
Holy as that where, long ago,
The Hebrew met his God !

"I have not caused the widow's tears
Nor dimmed the orphan's eye,
I have not stained the virgin's years,
Nor mocked the mourner's cry ;
The songs of Zion, in mine ear,
Have ever been most sweet,
And always when I felt Thee near,
My 'shoes' were 'off my feet.'

"I have known Thee, in the whirlwind,
I have known Thee, on the hill,
I have loved Thee, in the voice of birds,
Or the music of the rill.
I dreamt Thee in the shadow,
I saw Thee in the light,
I heard Thee in the thunder-peal,
And worshipped in the night.
All beauty, while it spoke of Thee,
Still made my soul rejoice,
And my spirit bowed within itself,
To hear Thy 'still-small voice.'
I *have* not felt myself a thing
Far from Thy presence driven,
By flaming sword or waving wing,
Shut out from Thee and heaven.

"Must I the whirlwind reap, because
My fathers sowed the storm,
Or shrink—because *another* sinned,—
Beneath Thy red right-arm?
O, much of this we dimly scan,
And much is all unknown,—
But I will not take my curse from *man*,
I turn to Thee, alone!
O, bid my fainting spirit live,
And what is dark reveal,
And what is evil O forgive,
And what is broken heal,
And cleanse my nature, from above,
In the deep Jordan of Thy love!

"I know not if the Christian's heaven
Shall be the same as mine,
I only ask to be forgiven,
And taken home to Thine.
I weary on a far, dim strand,
Whose mansions are as tombs,
And long to find the fatherland
Where there are many homes.
O grant, of all yon starry thrones,
Some dim and distant star,
Where Judah's lost and scattered sons
May love Thee, from afar!
When all earth's myriad harps shall meet,
In choral praise and prayer,
Shall Zion's harp—of old, so sweet—
Alone be wanting there?
Yet, place me in Thy lowest seat,
Though I—as now—be there
The Christian's scorn, the Christian's jest;
But let me see and hear,
From some dim mansion, in the sky,
Thy bright ones, and their melody!"

The sun goes down, with sudden gleam,
And—beautiful as a lovely dream,
And silently as air—
The vision of a dark-eyed girl,
With long and raven hair,
Glides in—as guardian spirits glide—
And, lo! is kneeling by his side;
As if her sudden presence there
Were sent, in answer to his prayer!

(O, say they not that angels tread
Around the good man's dying-bed?)
His child!—his sweet and sinless child!—
And as he gazed on her,
He knew his God was reconciled,
And this the messenger,—
As sure as God had hung, on high,
The promise-bow before his eye!—
Earth's purest hope thus o'er him flung,
To point his heavenward faith,
And life's most holy feeling strung,
To sing him into death!—
And, on his daughter's stainless breast,
The dying Hebrew sought his rest!

The Devil turned uneasily round,
For he knew that the place was holy ground!
But, ere he passed, he saw a Turk
Spit on the bearded Jew;
And a Christian cursed those who could not eat
    pork;—
Quoth the Devil, "These worthies may do my
    work;
For one lost, here are two!
Turk or Jew, or their Christian brother,
I seldom lose one, but I gain another!"

                    THOMAS KEBLE HERVEY

89

A JEWISH FAMILY

Genius of Raphael! if thy wings
  Might bear thee to this glen,
With faithful memory left of things
  To pencil dear and pen,
Thou wouldst forego the neighboring Rhine,
  And all his majesty—
A studious forehead to incline
  O'er this poor family.

The Mother—her thou must have seen,
  In spirit, ere she came
To dwell these rifted rocks between,
  Or found on earth a name;
An image, too, of that sweet Boy,
  Thy inspirations give—
Of playfulness, and love, and joy,
  Predestined here to live.

Downcast or shooting glances far,
  How beautiful his eyes,
That blend the nature of the star
  With that of summer skies!
I speak as if of sense beguiled;
  Uncounted months have gone,
Yet am I with the Jewish Child,
  That exquisite Saint John,

I see the dark brown curls, the brow,
　The smooth, transparent skin,
Refined, as with intent to show
　The holiness within;
The grace of parting Infancy
　By blushes yet untamed;
Age faithful to the mother's knee,
　Nor of her arms ashamed.

Two lovely sisters, still and sweet
　As flowers, stand side by side;
Their soul-subduing looks might cheat
　The Christian of his pride:
Such beauty hath the Eternal poured
　Upon them not forlorn,
Though of a lineage once abhorred,
　Nor yet redeemed from scorn.

Mysterious safeguard, that, in spite
　Of poverty and wrong,
Doth here preserve a living light,
　From Hebrew fountains sprung;
That gives this ragged group to cast
　Around the dell a gleam
Of Palestine, of glory past,
　And proud Jerusalem.

　　　　　　　　WILLIAM WORDSWORTH

90
THE WEEK
(From *Bible Characters*)

　The period of time, a week, and its universal existence, is a monumental proof of the truth of

Moses. Years, months and days are derivable from the sun and moon; but the week is an unnatural division. Yet there never was an age when it did not prevail in India, China, Assyria, Egypt, and it migrated to Greece and Rome. The world is large, and full of conflicting opinions. How many solutions exist of this arbitrary division—seven days! There is only one known to creation that is adequate, for it says the parents of all mankind were taught it by their Creator. Now try any other solution and it will be found inadequate, and evidently to accept an inadequate solution of an undeniable fact is credulity in one of its weakest forms.

CHARLES READE

91

FRIDAY NIGHT

On Sabbath Eve—thus have the sages said—
Man's homeward path, with him, two spirits tread.

The one a holy angel, pure and bright,
And one, a demon of malignant spite.

Happy the dwelling, where the day of rest
Is fitly honored as a welcome guest:

Where Sabbath-lamp doth hallowed radiance shed
Above the board, with festal dainties spread:

Where grateful hearts have sung with glad acclaim
Hymns of thanksgiving to God's holy name.

With sacred joy, the messenger of light,
With inward raging, the malignant sprite,

Behold. The first in tones serene and clear
Echoes the rapture of the ancient seer:

"How lovely are the tents of Jacob's race;
Israel, how beautiful thy dwelling place!"

"Amen!" the other with ungracious mien,
Responds; and turns to fly th' unwelcome scene;

But heareth, even though he hasten flight,
In fervent blessing raised, that voice of light.

"Be every Sabbath blessed as this!" Again,
Despite his will, the demon cries, "Amen!"

But woe the household, that the holy eve
Finds unprepared its presence to receive:

The lamp unlighted, table unadorned,
With work unhallowed, God's sweet Sabbath
    scorned:

Where no glad heart hath chanted "Come, O
    Bride!"
—Ah, woe, that thrice unhappy home betide.

Weeping, the radiant angel leaves the place
Where all unwelcome is his holy face.

The Demon of Unrest, with joy malign,
Sees him depart; and cries "This house is mine!"

"Be Sabbath-joys forever here unknown!"
"Amen!" he hears the angel's farewell moan.

O, blessed Sabbath, of God's gifts the best,
O, Royal Bride! O, lovely Queen of Rest,

Our lamp is lighted, and its sacred flame
Shines to thy glory and thy Monarch's name.

In grateful melody, our voice we raise
To sing thy beauty and thy Maker's praise.

Would all God's people knew thy saving grace,
And thou, in all their hearts, held'st honored place.

Would all God's people, in the blessings rare
Thy loyal ones enjoy, might weekly share!

For though stern Woe rule all the world besides,
Where Sabbath dwells, there happiness abides!

"Then come, who art thy husband's crown, in peace;
Our sorrows lighten, and our joys increase."

"Amid the faithful whom thy love hath blessed,
Come, beauteous Bride! Come, gracious Queen of Rest!"

SOLOMON SOLIS-COHEN

92

THE SABBATH

(From *The Genius of Judaism*)

An entire cessation from all the affairs of life on each seventh day is a Jewish institution, and is not prescribed by the laws of any other people. . . .

So inviolable was held the sanctity of this day, that its uninterrupted course was preferred to the preservation of life itself, of which history has recorded some instances of the most solemn nature, and some whose result has been not a little ludicrous.

. . . .

To the ancient Polytheists, nothing seemed so joyless as the austerity of a Jewish Sabbath. It was a strange abandonment of all the vocations of life. They saw the fields of the Hebrew forsaken by the laborer; the ass unsaddled; the oar laid by in the boat; they marked a dead stillness pervading the habitation of the Israelite; the fire extinguished, the meat unprepared, the man servant and the maiden leave their work, and the trafficker, at least one day of the week, refusing the offered coin. When the Hebrews had armies of their own, they would halt in the midst of victory on the eve of the Sabbath, and on the Sabbath day ceased even to defend their walls from the incursions of an enemy.

. . . .

The primitive Christians abhorred the observances of the Jewish Sabbath, which they considered as only practised by the contemners of "the Lord's day." . . . . . .

The interior delights of the habitation of the Hebrew were alike invisible to the Polytheist and the Christian fathers. They heard not the domestic greetings which cheerfully announced "the good Sabbath," nor the paternal benediction for the sons, nor the blessing of the master for his pupils. They could not behold the mistress of the house watching the sunset, and then lighting the seven wicks of the lamps of the Sabbath suspended during its consecration; for oil to fill the Sabbath-lamp, the mendicant implored an alms. But the more secret illumination of the law on the Sabbath, as the Rabbins expressed it, bestowed a supernumerary soul on every Israelite. The sanctity felt through the Jewish abode on that day, was an unfailing renewal of the religious emotions of this pious race. Thus in the busy circle of life was there one unmovable point where the weary rested, and the wealthy enjoyed a heavenly repose.

. . . .

It is beautiful to trace the expansion of an original and vast idea in the mind of a rare character who seems born to govern the human race. Such an awful and severe genius was the legislator of the Hebrews. The Sabbatical institution he boldly extended to a seventh year, equally as he had appointed a seventh day. At that periodical return the earth was suffered to lie fallow and at rest. In this "Sabbath of the land," the Hebrews were not permitted to plant, to sow, or to reap; and of the spontaneous growth no proprietor at those seasons was allowed to gather more than sufficed for the bare maintenance of his household. There was also release of debtors. The sublime genius of Moses looked far into futurity when, extending this great moral influence, he planned the still greater Sabbatical institution for every fifty years. Seven Sabbaths of years closed in the Jubilee, or the great year of release. Then at the blowing of the horn in the synagogue the poor man ceased to want; the slave was freed; all pledges were returned; and all lands reverted to their original proprietors. To prevent an excessive accumulation of wealth, the increase of unlimited debts, and the perpetuity of slavery, this creator of a political institution like no other, decreed that nothing should be perpetual but the religious republic itself.

ISAAC DISRAELI

93

SABBATH IN THE JEWISH CAMP

(From *Alroy*)

When the sun set, the Sabbath was to commence. The undulating horizon rendered it difficult to ascertain the precise moment of his fall. The crimson orb sunk behind the purple mountains, the sky was flushed with a rich and rosy glow. Then might be perceived the zealots, proud in their Talmudical lore, holding a skein of white silk in their hands, and announcing the approach of the Sabbath by their observation of its shifting tints. While the skein was yet golden, the forge of the armorer still sounded, the fire of the cook still blazed, still the cavalry led their steeds to the river, and still the busy footmen braced up their tents, and hammered at their palisades. The skein of silk became rosy, the armorer worked with renewed energy, the cook puffed with increased zeal, the horsemen scampered from the river, the footmen cast an anxious glance at the fading twilight.

The skein of silk became blue; a dim, dull, sepulchral, leaden tinge fell over its purity. The hum of gnats arose, the bat flew in circling whirls over the tents, horns sounded from all quarters, the sun had set, the Sabbath had commenced. The forge was mute, the fire extinguished, the prance of horses and the bustle of men in a moment ceased. A deep, a sudden, an all-pervading stillness dropped over that mighty host. It was night; the sacred lamp of the Sabbath sparkled in every tent of the camp, which vied in silence and in brilliancy with the mute and glowing heavens.

Morn came; the warriors assembled around the altar and the sacrifice. The High Priest and his attendant Levites proclaimed the unity and the omnipotence of the God of Israel, and the sympathetic responses of his conquering and chosen people re-echoed over the plain. They retired again to their tents, to listen to the expounding of the law; even the distance of a Sabbath walk was not to exceed that space which lies between Jerusalem and the Mount of Olives. This was the distance between the temple and the tabernacle, it had been nicely measured, and every Hebrew who ventured forth from the camp this day might be observed counting the steps of a Sabbath-day's journey. At length the sun again set, and on a sudden fires blazed, voices sounded, men stirred, in the same enchanted and instantaneous manner that had characterized the stillness of the preceding eve. Shouts of laughter, bursts of music, announced the festivity of the coming night; supplies poured in from all the neighboring villages, and soon the pious conquerors commemorated their late triumph in a round of banqueting.

BENJAMIN DISRAELI

94

ODE TO ZION

Art thou not, Zion, fain
To send forth greetings from thy sacred rock
Unto thy captive train,
Who greet thee as the remnants of thy flock?
Take thou on every side—
East, west, and south, and north—their greetings
    multiplied.
Sadly he greets thee still,
The prisoner of hope, who, day and night,
Shed ceaseless tears, like dew on Hermon's hill—
Would that they fell upon thy mountain's height!

Harsh is my voice when I bewail thy woes,
But when in fancy's dream
I see thy freedom, forth its cadence flows
Sweet as the harps that hung by Babel's stream.
My heart is sore distressed
For Bethel ever blessed,
For Peniel, and each ancient, sacred place.
The holy presence there
To thee is present where
Thy Maker opes thy gates, the gates of heaven to face.

The glory of the Lord will ever be
Thy sole and perfect light;
No need hast thou, then, to illumine thee,
Of sun by day, and moon and stars by night.
I would that, where God's Spirit was of yore
Poured out unto thy holy ones, I might
There too my soul outpour!
The house of kings and throne of God wert thou,
How comes it then that now
Slaves fill the throne where sat thy kings before?

O! who will lead me on
To seek the spots where, in far-distant years,
The angels in their glory dawned upon
Thy messengers and seers?
O! who will give me wings
That I may fly away,
And there, at rest from all my wanderings,
The ruins of my heart among thy ruins lay?
I'll bend my face unto thy soil, and hold
Thy stones as precious gold.

And when in Hebron I have stood beside
My fathers' tombs, then will I pass in turn
Thy plains and forest wide,
Until I stand on Gilead and discern
Mount Hor and Mount Abarim, 'neath whose crest
Thy luminaries twain, thy guides and beacons rest.

Thy air is life unto my soul, thy grains
Of dust are myrrh, thy streams with honey flow;
Naked and barefoot, to thy ruined fanes
How gladly would I go;
To where the ark was treasured, and in dim
Recesses dwelt the holy cherubim.

I rend the beauty of my locks, and cry
In bitter wrath against the cruel fate
That bids thy holy Nazarites to lie
In earth contaminate.
How can I make or meat or drink my care,
How can mine eyes enjoy
The light of day, when I see ravens tear
Thy eagles' flesh, and dogs thy lions' whelps destroy?
Away! thou cup of sorrow's poisoned gall!
Scarce can my soul thy bitterness sustain.
When I Ahola unto mind recall,
I taste thy venom; and when once again
Upon Aholiba I muse, thy dregs I drain.

Perfect in beauty, Zion! how in thee
Do love and grace unite!
The souls of thy companions tenderly
Turn unto thee; thy joy was their delight,

And, weeping, they lament thy ruin now.
In distant exile, for thy sacred height
They long, and towards thy gates in prayer they
    bow.
Thy flocks are scattered o'er the barren waste,
Yet do they not forget thy sheltering fold,
Unto thy garment's fringe they cling, and haste
The branches of thy palms to seize and hold.

Shinar and Pathros! come they near to thee?
Naught are they by thy Light and Right divine.
To what can be compared the majesty
Of thy anointed line?
To what the singers, seers, and Levites thine?
The rule of idols fails and is cast down,
Thy power eternal is, from age to age, thy crown.

The Lord desires thee for his dwelling place
Eternally; and blest
Is he whom God has chosen for the grace
Within thy courts to rest.
Happy is he that watches, drawing near,
Until he sees thy glorious lights arise,
And over whom thy dawn breaks full and clear
Set in the Orient skies.
But happiest he, who, with exultant eyes,
The bliss of thy redeemed ones shall behold,
And see thy youth renewed as in the days of old.

JEHUDA HALEVI
Translation from the Hebrew by Mrs. Henry Lucas

95

SABBATH, MY LOVE

I greet my love with wine and gladsome lay;
Welcome, thrice welcome, joyous Seventh Day!

Six slaves the week days are; I share
With them a round of toil and care,
Yet light the burdens seem, I bear
      For thy sweet sake, Sabbath my love!

On Sunday, to the accustomed task
I go content, nor guerdon ask
Save in thy smile, at length, to bask—
      Day blessed of God, Sabbath my love!

Is Monday dull, Tuesday unbright?
Hide sun and stars from Wednesday's sight?
What need I care, who have thy light,
      Orb of my life, Sabbath my love!

The fifth day, joyful tidings ring:
"The morrow shall thy freedom bring!"
At dawn a slave, at eve a king—
      God's table waits, Sabbath my love!

On Friday doth my cup o'erflow,
What blissful rest the night shall know
When, in thine arms, my toil and woe
      Are all forgot, Sabbath my love!

'Tis dusk. With sudden light, distilled
From one sweet face, the world is filled ;
The tumult of my heart is stilled—
  For thou art come, Sabbath my love!

Bring fruits and wine and sing a gladsome lay,
Cry "Come in peace, O restful Seventh Day!"

JEHUDA HALEVI
Free translation from the Hebrew by Solomon Solis-Cohen

96

THE HARVEST FESTIVAL

(*Succoth*—From *Tancred*)

The feast of tabernacles shalt thou hold for thyself seven days, when thou hast gathered in the produce of thy threshing floor and of thy wine-press.—DEUTERONOMY xvi. 13.

And ye shall take unto yourselves on the first day the fruit of the tree hadar, branches of palm trees, and the boughs of the myrtle tree, and willows of the brook ; and ye shall rejoice before the Lord your God seven days.—LEVITICUS xxiii. 40.

The vineyards of Israel have ceased to exist, but the eternal law enjoins the children of Israel still to celebrate the vintage. A race that persist in celebrating their vintage, although they have no fruits to gather, will regain their vineyards. What sublime inexorability in the law! But what indomitable spirit in the people.

It is easy for the happier Sephardim, the Hebrews who have never quitted the sunny regions that are laved by the Midland Ocean,—it is easy for them, though they have lost their heritage, to sympathize, in their beautiful Asian cities, or in their Moorish and Arabian gardens, with the graceful rites that are, at least, an homage to a benignant nature. But picture to yourself the child of Israel in the dingy suburb or the squalid quarter of some bleak northern town, where there is never a sun that can at any rate ripen grapes. Yet he must celebrate the vintage of purple Palestine! The law has told him, though a denizen in an icy clime, that he must dwell for seven days in a bower, and that he must build it of the boughs of thick trees; and the Rabbins have told him that these thick trees are the palm, the myrtle, and the weeping willow. Even Sarmatia may furnish a weeping willow. The law has told him that he must pluck the fruit of goodly trees, and the Rabbins have explained that the goodly fruit on this occasion is confined to the citron. . . . .

His mercantile connections will enable him, often at considerable cost, to procure some palm leaves from Canaan which he may wave in his synagogue, while he exclaims, ...

"Hosannah, in the highest!"

There is something profoundly interesting in this devoted observance of Oriental customs in the heart of our Saxon and Sclavonian cities; in these descendants of the Bedoueens, who conquered Canaan more than three thousand years ago, still celebrating that success which secured their forefathers for the first time grapes and wine.

Conceive a being born and bred in the Judenstrasse of Hamburg or Frankfort, or rather in the purlieus of our Houndsditch or Minories, born to hereditary insult, without any education, apparently without a circumstance that can develop the slightest taste or cherish the least sentiment for the beautiful, living amid fogs and filth, never treated with kindness, seldom with justice, occupied with the meanest, if not the vilest, toil, bargaining for frippery, speculating in usury, under the concurrent influences of degrading causes which would have worn out long ago any race that was not of the unmixed blood of Caucasus, and did not adhere to the laws of Moses—conceive such a being, an object to you of prejudice, dislike, disgust, perhaps hatred. The season arrives, and the mind and heart of that being are filled with images and passions that have been ranked in all ages among the most beautiful and the most genial of human experience; filled with a subject the most vivid, the most graceful, the most joyous, and the most exuberant—a subject that has inspired poets, and which has made gods—the harvest of the grape in the native regions of the Vine.

He rises in the morning, goes early to some Whitechapel market, purchases some willow boughs for which he has previously given a commission, and which are brought probably from one of the neighboring rivers of Essex, hastens home, cleans out the yard of his miserable tenement, builds his bower, decks it, even profusely, with the finest flowers and fruits that he can procure, the myrtle and the citron never forgotten, and hangs its roof with variegated lamps. After the service of his Synagogue, he sups late with his wife and his children in the open air, as if he were in the pleasant villages of Galilee, beneath its sweet and starry sky.

Perhaps, as he is giving the Keedush, the Hebrew blessing to the Hebrew meal, breaking and distributing the bread, and sanctifying with a preliminary prayer the goblet of wine he holds, . . or perhaps as he is offering up the peculiar thanksgiving of the Feast of Tabernacles, praising Jehovah for the vintage which his children may no longer cull, but also for his promise that they may some day again enjoy it, and his wife and his children are joining in a pious Hosannah—that is, Save us!—a party of Anglo-Saxons, very respectable men, ten-pounders, a little elevated it may be, though certainly not in honor of the vintage, pass the house, and words like these are heard:

"I say, Buggins, what's that row?"

"Oh! it's those cursed Jews! we've a lot of 'em here. It is one of their horrible feasts. The Lord Mayor ought to interfere However, things are not as bad as they used to be; they used always to crucify little boys at these hullabaloos, but now they only eat sausages made of stinking pork."

"To be sure," replies his companion, "we all make progress."

BENJAMIN DISRAELI

ISRAEL AND HIS REVELATION

(From *Literature and Dogma*)

The whole history of the world to this day is in truth one continual establishing of the Old Testament revelation: *O ye that love the Eternal, see that ye hate the thing that is evil! to him that ordereth his conversation right, shall be shown the salvation of God.* And whether we consider this revelation in respect to human affairs at large, or in respect to individual happiness, in either case its importance is so immense, that the people to whom it was given, and whose record is in the Bible, deserve fully to be singled out as the Bible singles them. "Behold, darkness shall cover the earth, and gross darkness the nations; but the Eternal shall arise upon *thee*, and his glory shall be seen upon thee!" For, while other nations had the misleading idea that this or that, other than righteousness, is saving, and it is not; that this or that, other than conduct, brings happiness, and it does not; Israel had the true idea that *righteousness* is saving, and that to *conduct* belongs happiness.

Nor let it be said that other nations, too, had at least something of this idea. They had, but they were not *possessed* with it; and to feel it enough to make the world feel it, it was necessary to be possessed with it. It is not sufficient to have been visited with such an idea at times, to have had it forced occasionally on one's mind by the teachings of experience. No; *he that hath the bride is the bridegroom;* the idea belongs to him who has most *loved* it. Common prudence can say: Honesty is the best policy; morality can say: To conduct belongs happiness. But Israel and the Bible are filled with religious joy, and rise higher and say: *"Righteousness is salvation!"* and this is what is inspiring. " I have *stuck* unto thy testimonies! Eternal what *love* have I unto thy law! *all the day long* is my study in it. Thy testimonies have I claimed as *mine heritage for ever,* and why? they are *the very joy of my heart!"* This is why the testimonies of righteousness are Israel's heritage forever, because they were *the very joy of his heart.* Herein Israel stood alone, the friend and elect of the Eternal. " He showeth his word unto *Jacob,* his statutes and ordinances unto *Israel.* He hath not dealt so with any nation, neither have the heathen knowledge of his laws."

MATTHEW ARNOLD

98

ISRAEL AS BRIDE AND AS BEGGAR

(From *Jews of Angevin England,* by Joseph Jacobs)

Erst radiant the Bride adored,
On whom rich wedding gifts are poured;
She weeps, sore wounded, overthrown,
Exiled and outcast, shunned and lone.

Laid all aside her garments fair,
The pledges of a bond divine,
A wandering beggar-woman's wear
Is hers in lieu of raiment fine.

Chaunted hath been in every land
The beauty of her crown and zone;
Now doomed, dethroned she maketh moan,
Bemocked—a byword—cursed and banned.

An airy, joyous step was hers
Beneath Thy wing. But now she crawls
Along and mourns her sons and errs
At every step, and, worn out, falls.

And yet to Thee she clingeth tight,
Vain, vain to her man's mortal might
Which in a breath to naught is hurled,
Thy smile alone makes up her world.

ELCHANAN
Translation by Israel Zangwill

(The acrostic informs us that this poem was written by Elchanan.)

99
"FORGIVEN"

(From *Jews of Angevin England*, by Joseph Jacobs)

Ay 'tis thus	Evil us	hath in bond;
By thy grace	guilt efface	and respond
		" Forgiven!"
Cast scorn o'er	and abhor	th' informer's word;
Dear God, deign	this refrain	to make heard
		" Forgiven!"

"FORGIVEN"

Ear in lieu	give him who	intercedes;
Favoring	answer, King,	when he pleads,
		"Forgiven!"
Grant also	the lily blow	in Abram's right;
Heal our shame	and proclaim	from thine height
		"Forgiven!"
Just forgiving,	Mercy living,	sin condone;
List our cry,	loud reply	from Thy Throne
		"Forgiven!"
My wound heal,	deep conceal	stain and flake,
Now gain praise	by Thy phrase	"For My sake,
		Forgiven!"
O forgive!	Thy sons live	from thee reft;
Praised for grace,	Turn thy face	to those left—
		"Forgiven!"
Raise to Thee	this my plea,	take my pray'r,
Sin unmake	for Thy sake	and declare,
		"Forgiven!"
Tears, regret,	witness set	in Sin's place;
Uplift trust	from the dust	to Thy face—
		"Forgiven!"
Voice that moans,	tears and groans,	do not spurn;
Weigh not flaws,	plead my cause,	and return,
		"Forgiven!"
Yea, off-rolled,	as foretold,	clouds impure,
Zion's folk,	free of yoke	O assure,
		"Forgiven!"
Day by day	stronghold they	seek in Thee,
Good One! let	stronger yet	Thy word be
		"Forgiven!"

YOMTOB OF YORK
Translation by Israel Zangwill

100

JEWISH NATIONALITY

(From *Daniel Deronda*)

"Well, whatever the Jews contributed at one time, they are a stand-still people," said Lilly. "They are the type of obstinate adherence to the superannuated. They may show good abilities when they take up liberal ideas, but as a race they have no development in them."

"That is false!" said Mordecai, leaning forward again with his former eagerness. "Let their history be known and examined; let the seed be sifted, let its beginning be traced to the weed of the wilderness—the more glorious will be the energy that transformed it. Where else is there a nation of whom it may be as truly said that their religion and law and moral life mingled as the stream of blood in the heart and made one growth—where else a people who kept and enlarged their spiritual store at the very time when they were hunted with a hatred as fierce as the forest-fires that chase the wild beast from his covert? There is a fable of the Roman, that, swimming to save his life, he held the roll of his writings between his teeth and saved them from the waters. But how much more than that is true of our race? They struggled to keep their place among the nations like heroes—yea, when the hand was hacked off, they clung with the teeth; but when the plow and the harrow had passed over the last visible signs of their national covenant, and the fruitfulness of their land was stifled with the blood of the sowers and planters, they said, 'The spirit is alive, let us make it a lasting habitation—lasting because movable—so that it may be carried from generation to generation, and our sons unborn may be rich in the things that have been, and possess a hope built on an unchangeable foundation.' They said it and they wrought it, though often breathing with scant life, as in a coffin, or as lying wounded amidst a heap of slain. Hooted and scared like the unowned dog, the Hebrew made himself envied for his wealth and wisdom, and was bled of them to fill the bath of Gentile luxury; he absorbed knowledge, he diffused it; his dispersed race was a new Phœnicia working the mines of Greece, and carrying their products to the world. The native spirit of our tradition was not to stand still, but to use records as a seed, and draw out the compressed virtues of law and prophecy; and while the Gentile, who had said, 'What is yours is ours, and no longer yours,' was reading the letter of our law as a dark inscription, or was turning its parchments into shoe-soles for an army rabid with lust and cruelty, our Masters were still enlarging and illuminating with fresh-fed interpretation. But the dispersion was wide, the yoke of oppression was a spiked torture as well as a load; the exile was forced afar among brutish people, where the consciousness of his race was no clearer to him than the light of the sun to our fathers in the Roman persecution, who had their hiding place in a cave, and knew not that it was day save by the dimmer burning of their candles. What wonder that multitudes of our people are ignorant, narrow, superstitious? What wonder?"

Here Mordecai, whose seat was near the fireplace, rose and leaned his arm on the little shelf; his excitement had risen, though his voice, which had begun with unusual strength, was getting hoarser.

"What wonder? The night is unto them, that they have no vision; in their darkness they are unable to divine; the sun is gone down over the prophets, and the day is dark above them; their observances are as nameless relics. But which among the chief of the Gentile nations has not an ignorant multitude? They scorn our people's ignorant observance; but the most accursed ignorance is that which has no observance—sunk to the cunning greed of the fox, to which all law is no more than a trap or the cry of the worrying hound. There is a degradation deep down below the memory that has withered into superstition. In the multitudes of the ignorant on three continents who observe our rites and make the confession of the Divine Unity, the soul of Judaism is not dead. Revive the organic centre: let the unity of Israel which has made the growth and form of its religion be an outward reality. Looking toward a land and a polity, our dispersed people in all ends of the earth may share the dignity of a national life which has a voice among the peoples of the East and the West—which will plant the wisdom and skill of our race so that it may be, as of old, a medium of transmission and understanding. Let that come to pass, and the living warmth will spread to the weak extremities of Israel, and superstition will vanish, not in the lawlessness of the renegade, but in the illumination of great facts which widen feeling, and make all knowledge alive as the young offspring of beloved memories."

. . . .

All eyes were fixed on Mordecai as he sat down again, and none with unkindness; but it happened that the one who felt the most kindly was the most prompted to speak in opposition. This was the genial and rational Gideon, who also was not without a sense that he was addressing the guest of the evening. He said:

"You have your own way of looking at things, Mordecai, and, as you say, your own way seems to you rational. I know you don't hold with the restoration to Judea, by miracle, and so on; but you are as well aware as I am that the subject has been mixed with a heap of nonsense both by Jews and Christians. And as to the connection of our race with Palestine, it has been perverted by superstition till it's as demoralizing as the old poor-law. The raff and scum go there to be maintained like able-bodied paupers, and to be taken special care of by the angel Gabriel when they die. It's no use fighting against facts. The most learned and liberal men among us who are attached to our religion are clearing our liturgy of all such notions as a literal fulfilment of the prophecies about restoration and so on. Prune it of a few useless rites and literal interpretations of that sort, and our religion is the simplest of all religions, and makes no barrier, but a union, between us and the rest of the world."

"As plain as a pike-staff," said Pash, with an ironical laugh. "You pluck it up by the roots, strip off the leaves and bark, shave off the knots, and smooth it at top and bottom; put it where you will, it will do no harm, it will never sprout. You may make a handle of it, or you may throw it on the bon-fire of scoured rubbish. I don't see why our rubbish is to be held sacred any more than the rubbish of Brahmanism or Buddhism."

"No," said Mordecai, "no, Pash, because you have lost the heart of the Jew. Community was felt before it was called good. I praise no superstition, I praise the living fountains of enlarging belief. What is growth, completion, development? You began with that question; I apply it to the history of our people. I say that the effect of our separateness will not be completed and have its highest transformation unless our race takes on again the character of a nationality. That is the fulfilment of the religious trust that moulded them into a people, whose life has made itself the inspiration of the world. What is it to me that the ten tribes are lost untraceably, or that multitudes of the children of Judah have mixed themselves with the Gentile populations as a river with rivers? Behold our people still! Their skirts spread afar; they are torn and soiled and trodden on; but there is a jeweled breastplate. Let the wealthy men, the monarchs of commerce, the learned in all knowledge, the skilful in all arts, the speakers, the political counsellors, who carry in their veins the Hebrew blood which has maintained its vigor in all climates, and the pliancy of the Hebrew genius for which difficulty means new device—let them say, 'We will lift up a standard, we will unite in a labor hard, but glorious, like that of Moses and Ezra, a labor which shall be a worthy fruit of the long anguish whereby our fathers maintained their separateness, refusing the ease of falsehood.' They have wealth enough to redeem the soil from debauched and paupered conquerors, they have the skill of the statesman to devise, the tongue of the orator to persuade. And is there no prophet or poet among us to make the ears of Christian Europe tingle with shame at the hideous obloquy of Christian strife, which the Turk gazes at as at the fighting of beasts to which he has lent an arena? There is store of wisdom among us to found a new Jewish polity, grand, simple, just, like the old—a republic where there is equality of protection, an equality that shone like a star on the forehead of our ancient community, and gave it more than the brightness of Western freedom amidst the despotisms of the East. Then our race shall have an organic centre, a heart and brain to watch and guide and execute; the outraged Jew shall have a defence in the court of nations, as the outraged Englishman or American. And the world will gain as Israel gains. For there will be a community in the van of the East which carries the culture and the sympathies of every nation in its bosom; there will be a land set for a halting-place of enmities, a neutral ground for the East as Belgium is for the West. Difficulties? I know there are difficulties. But let the spirit of sublime achievement move in the great among our people, and the work will begin."

. . . .

"It may seem well enough on one side to make so much of our memories and inheritance as you do, Mordecai," said Gideon; "but there's another side. It isn't all gratitude and harmless glory. Our people have inherited a good deal of hatred. There's a pretty lot of curses still flying about, and stiff, settled rancor, inherited from the times of persecution. How will you justify keeping one sort of memory and throwing away the other? There are ugly debts standing on both sides."

"I justify the choice as all other choice is justified," said Mordecai, "I cherish nothing for the Jewish nation, I seek nothing for them, but the good which promises good to all the nations. The spirit of our religious life, which is one with our national life, is not hatred of aught but wrong. The masters have said, an offence against man is worse than an offence against God. But what wonder if there is hatred in the breasts of Jews, who are children of the ignorant and oppressed—what wonder, since there is hatred in the breasts of Christians? Our national life was a growing light. Let the central fire be kindled again, and the light will reach afar. The degraded and scorned of our race will learn to think of their sacred land, not as a place for saintly beggary to await death in loathsome idleness, but as a republic where the Jewish spirit manifests itself in a new order founded on the old, purified, enriched by the experience our greatest sons have gathered from the life of the ages. How long is it?—only two centuries since a vessel carried over the ocean the beginning of the great North American nation. The people grew like meeting waters. They were various in habit and sect. There came a time, a century ago, when they needed a polity, and there were heroes of peace among them. What had they to form a polity with but memories of Europe, corrected by the vision of a better? Let our wise and wealthy show themselves heroes. They have the memories of the East and West, and they have the full vision of a better. A new Persia with a purified religion magnified itself in art and wisdom. So with a new Judea, poised between East and West—a covenant of reconciliation. Will any say, the prophetic vision of your race has been hopelessly mixed with folly and bigotry ; the angel of progress has no message for Judaism— it is a half-buried city for the paid workers to lay open—the waters are rushing by it as a forsaken field? I say that the strongest principle of growth lies in human choice. The sons of Judah have to choose, that God may again choose them. The Messianic time is the time when Israel shall will the planting of the national ensign. The Nile overflowed and rushed onward : the Egyptian could not choose the overflow, but he chose to work and make channels for the fructifying waters, and Egypt became the land of corn. Shall man, whose soul is set in the royalty of discernment and resolve, deny his rank, and say, 'I am an onlooker; ask no choice or purpose of me?' That is the blasphemy of his time. The divine principle of our race is action, choice, resolved memory. Let us contradict the blasphemy, and help to will our own better future and the better future of the world—not renounce our higher gift, and say, ' Let us be as if we were not among the populations;' but choose our full heritage, claim the brotherhood of our nation, and carry into it a new brotherhood with the nations of the Gentiles. The vision is there; it will be fulfilled."

GEORGE ELIOT

And here will I make an end.

And if I have done well, and as is fitting the story, it is that which I desired; but if slenderly and meanly, it is that which I could attain unto.

For as it is hurtful to drink wine or water alone; and as wine mingled with water is pleasant, and delighteth the taste; even so, speech finely framed delighteth the ears of them that read the story.

And here shall be an end.

—2 MACCABEES xv. 37-39.

INDEX OF AUTHORS

(The figures refer to the numbers of the selections)

Addison, Joseph, 12
Aguilar, Grace. 65
Aldrich, Thomas Bailey. 58, 74
Alexander, C. F., 25
Arnold, Edwin, 16, 17. 68
Arnold, Matthew, 97
Bonar, Horatius, 24
Borthwick, J. D., 32
Browne, Frances, 85
Browning, Robert, 33
Bryant, William Cullen, 13, 27
Byron, George Gordon Noel, 2, 35, 36, 46, 51, 54, 67
Campbell, 44
Cohen, Solomon Solis, 66, 91
Disraeli, Benjamin, 41, 77, 93, 96
Disraeli, Isaac, 72, 92
Drayton, Michael, 53, 59
Elchanan, 98
Eliot, George (Evans, Mary Ann C.), 100
Heber, Reginald, 22

Herbert, George, 4
Hervey, Thomas Keble. 88
Hood, Thomas, 31
Humboldt, von, Alexander, 10
Hunt, Leigh, 18
Jackson, George Anson. 57
Jehuda Halevi, 94, 95
Joseph (Rabbi), 70
Kalonymos ben Jehuda. 71
Kaufmann, David, 1
Lazarus, Emma, 69, 75, 76, 81, 82
Longfellow, Henry Wadsworth, 40, 62, 63, 64. 83, 84
Macaulay, Thomas Babington, 79. 80
Mackay, Charles. 15
Milton, John, 3, 14, 30, 49
Montgomery, James, 5, 6, 8
Moore, Thomas, 11, 26, 52
Plumptre, E. H., 34. 42
Priestley, Joseph, 78
Proctor, Bryan Waller, 55
Reade, Charles, 50, 60, 61, 90

Richardson, Benjamin Ward, 87
Scott, Sir Walter, 9, 73
Smith, Elizabeth Oakes, 47
Whittier, John Greenleaf, 19, 29, 56, 86
Wordsworth, William, 89
Yomtob of York, 99

Bible—Leeser's Translation, 20, 21, 39, 48
Bible—Revised Version, 7, 23, 28, 37
Hebrew Review, The, 38, 43, 45

INDEX OF SUBJECTS

(The figures refer to the numbers of the selections)

Abraham and the Fire-Worshipper, 18
Abraham's Bread, 17
Azar and Abraham, 16
Azrael, 40
Banner of the Jew, The, 82
Bar Kochba, 69
Battle of Beth-Horon, The, 64
Belshazzar, 55
Benjamin accompanies his Brethren to Egypt, 20
Burial of Moses, 25
But who shall see, 52
By the Rivers of Babylon we sat down and wept, 51
Captivity, The, 50
Child Samuel, The, 32
Cities of the Plain, The, 19
Civil Disabilities of the Jews, 79, 80
Crowing of the Red Cock, The, 81
David's Lament over Saul and Jonathan, 37
Death of Samson, 30
Deborah's Song, 28
Dedication of the Temple, The, 39
Descriptions of Nature in the Hebrew Writers, 10
Dying Hebrew's Prayer, The, 88
Elijah, 45
Elijah's Interview, 44
Exhortation to the Jews of Nordhausen, 76
Expulsion of the Jews from Spain, The, 77
Ezekiel, 56
False Gods, The, 49
First Crusade, The, 71
Forgiven, 99
Friday Night, 91
Future of Judaism, The, 1
Harp the Monarch Minstrel swept, The, 2
Harvest Festival, The, 96
Idolatry, 48

In Exile, 70
Israel and his Revelation, 97
Israel as Bride and as Beggar, 98
Jewish Captive, The, 47
Jewish Family, A, 89
Jewish Nationality, 100
Jew's Gift, The, 74
Jews of York, The, 72
Joseph and his Brethren, 21
Judas Maccabæus, 63
Judith and Holofernes, 58
Legend of Iyob the Upright, 57
Legend of Paradise, A, 87
Legend of Rabbi Ben Levi, The, 83
Lines for the Ninth of Ab, 66
Máhala and her Seven Sons, 62
Mount Hor, 24
Nehemiah, 60
Nehemiah, Reformer, 61
"No Man knoweth of his Sepulchre," 27
Ode to Zion, 94
Of the Prophecies concerning the Dispersion and Restoration of the Jews, 78
Oh! Weep for those, 46
Ozair the Jew, 68
Passage of the Red Sea, 22
Pharisees, The, 65
Plea for the Jews before the Council at Nordhausen, 75
Pools of Solomon, The, 41
Prayer of Mardocheus, The, 59
Prayer of Tobias, A, 53

Psalm IV, 3
Psalm XXIII, 4
Psalm XXVII, 5
Psalm XLII, 6
Psalm LXXX, 7
Psalm CXXI, 8
Queen of the South, The, 42
Rabbi's Vision, The, 85
Raising of Samuel, The, 35
Ruth, 31
Sabbath in the Jewish Camp, 93
Sabbath, my Love, 95
Sabbath, The, 92
Sandalphon, 84
Saul, 33
Solomon, The Youthful and the Aged, 43
Song of Moses, 23
Song of Rebecca the Jewess, 9
Song of Saul before his Last Battle, 36
Song of the Stars, 13
Songs of the Night, The, 38
Spacious Firmament on High, The, 12
Thou art, O God, 11
Trial of Rebecca, 73
Tubal Cain, 15
Two Rabbins, The, 86
View of Paradise, 14
Vision of Belshazzar, 54
Water of Bethlehem Gate, The, 34
Week, The, 90
Weep, Children of Israel, 26
Wife of Manoah, The, to her Husband, 29
Wild Gazelle, The, 67

PUBLICATIONS
OF THE
Jewish Publication Society
OF AMERICA.

OUTLINES OF JEWISH HISTORY. From the Return from Babylon to the Present Time. By Lady Magnus. (Revised by M. Friedländer.)
THINK AND THANK. By Samuel W. Cooper.
RABBI AND PRIEST. By Milton Goldsmith.
THE PERSECUTION OF THE JEWS IN RUSSIA.
VOEGELE'S MARRIAGE AND OTHER TALES. By Louis Schnabel.
CHILDREN OF THE GHETTO: BEING PICTURES OF A PECULIAR PEOPLE. By I. Zangwill.
SOME JEWISH WOMEN. By Henry Zirndorf.
HISTORY OF THE JEWS. By Prof. H. Graetz.
    Vol. I.   From the Earliest Period to the Death of Simon the Maccabee (135 B. C. E.).
    Vol. II.   From the Reign of Hyrcanus to the Completion of the Babylonian Talmud (500 C. E.).
    Vol. III.   From the Completion of the Babylonian Talmud to the Expulsion of the Jews from England (1290 C. E.).
    Vol. IV.   From the Rise of the Kabbala (1270 C. E.) to the Permanent Settlement of the Marranos in Holland (1618 C. E.).
    Vol. V.   From the Chmielnicki Persecution in Poland (1648 C. E.) to the Present Time. (In press.)
SABBATH HOURS. Thoughts. By Liebman Adler.
PAPERS OF THE JEWISH WOMEN'S CONGRESS.
OLD EUROPEAN JEWRIES. By David Philipson, D.D.
JEWISH LITERATURE AND OTHER ESSAYS. By Gustav Karpeles.
THE TALMUD. By Emanuel Deutsch.
READINGS AND RECITATIONS. Compiled by Isabel E. Cohen.

Dues, $3.00 per Annum.

ALL PUBLICATIONS FOR SALE BY THE TRADE AND AT THE SOCIETY'S OFFICE.

SPECIAL TERMS TO SCHOOLS AND LIBRARIES.

The Jewish Publication Society of America,
Office, 1015 Arch St.

P. O. BOX 1164.   PHILADELPHIA, PA.

OUTLINES OF JEWISH HISTORY.
From the Return from Babylon to the Present Time,
1890.
With Three Maps, a Frontispiece and Chronological Tables.

BY LADY MAGNUS.
REVISED BY M. FRIEDLÄNDER, PH. D.

OPINIONS OF THE PRESS.

The entire work is one of great interest; it is written with moderation, and yet with a fine enthusiasm for the great race which is set before the reader's mind —*Atlantic Monthly.*

We doubt whether there is in the English language a better sketch of Jewish history. The Jewish Publication Society is to be congratulated on the successful opening of its career. Such a movement, so auspiciously begun, deserves the hearty support of the public.—*Nation* (New York).

Of universal historical interest.—*Philadelphia Ledger.*

Compresses much in simple language.—*Baltimore Sun.*

Though full of sympathy for her own people, it is not without a singular value for readers whose religious belief differs from that of the author.—*New York Times.*

One of the clearest and most compact works of its class produced in modern times.—*New York Sun.*

The Jewish Publication Society of America has not only conferred a favor upon all young Hebrews, but also upon all Gentiles who desire to see the Jew as he appears to himself.—*Boston Herald.*

We know of no single-volume history which gives a better idea of the remarkable part played by the Jews in ancient and modern history.—*San Francisco Chronicle.*

A succinct, well-written history of a wonderful race.—*Buffalo Courier.*

The best hand-book of Jewish history that readers of any class can find.—*New York Herald.*

A convenient and attractive hand-book of Jewish history.—*Cleveland Plain Dealer.*

The work is an admirable one, and as a manual of Jewish history it may be commended to persons of every race and creed.—*Philadelphia Times.*

Altogether it would be difficult to find another book on this subject containing so much information.—*American* (Philadelphia).

Lady Magnus' book is a valuable addition to the store-house of literature that we already have about the Jews.—*Charleston (S. C.) News.*

We should like to see this volume in the library of every school in the State.—*Albany Argus.*

A succinct, helpful portrayal of Jewish history.—*Boston Post.*

Bound in Cloth.   Price, postpaid, $1.00, Library Edition.
75 cents, School Edition.

"THINK AND THANK."

A Tale for the Young, Narrating in Romantic Form the Boyhood of Sir Moses Montefiore.

WITH SIX ILLUSTRATIONS.

By SAMUEL W. COOPER.

OPINIONS OF THE PRESS.

A graphic and interesting story, full of incident and adventure, with an admirable spirit attending it consonant with the kindly and sweet, though courageous and energetic temper of the distinguished philanthropist.—*American* (Philadelphia).

THINK AND THANK is a most useful corrective to race prejudice. It is also deeply interesting as a biographical sketch of a distinguished Englishman.—*Philadelphia Ledger*.

A fine book for boys of any class to read.—*Public Opinion* (Washington).

It will have especial interest for the boys of his race, but all schoolboys can well afford to read it and profit by it.—*Albany Evening Journal*.

Told simply and well.—*New York Sun*.

An excellent story for children.—*Indianapolis Journal*.

The old as well as the young may learn a lesson from it.—*Jewish Exponent*.

It is a thrilling story exceedingly well told.—*American Israelite*.

The book is written in a plain, simple style, and is well adapted for Sunday-school libraries.—*Jewish Spectator*.

It is one of the very few books in the English language which can be placed in the hands of a Jewish boy with the assurance of arousing and maintaining his interest.—*Hebrew Journal*.

Intended for the young, but may well be read by their elders.—*Detroit Free Press*.

Bright and attractive reading.—*Philadelphia Press*.

THINK AND THANK will please boys, and it will be found popular in Sunday-school libraries.—*New York Herald*.

The story is a beautiful one, and gives a clear insight into the circumstances, the training and the motives that gave impulse and energy to the life-work of the great philanthropist.—*Kansas City Times*.

We should be glad to know that this little book has a large circulation among Gentiles as well as among the "chosen people." It has no trace of religious bigotry about it, and its perusal cannot but serve to make Christian and Jew better known to each other.—*Philadelphia Telegraph*.

Bound in Cloth.   **Price, postpaid, 50c.**

RABBI AND PRIEST.
A STORY.
BY MILTON GOLDSMITH.

OPINIONS OF THE PRESS.

The author has attempted to depict faithfully the customs and practices of the Russian people and government in connection with the Jewish population of that country. The book is a strong and well written story. We read and suffer with the sufferers.—*Public Opinion* (Washington).

Although addressed to Jews, with an appeal to them to seek freedom and peace in America, it ought to be read by humane people of all races and religions. Mr. Goldsmith is a master of English, and his pure style is one of the real pleasures of the story.—*Philadelphia Bulletin.*

The book has the merit of being well written, is highly entertaining, and it cannot fail to prove of interest to all who may want to acquaint themselves in the matter of the condition of affairs that has recently been attracting universal attention.—*San Francisco Call.*

RABBI AND PRIEST has genuine worth, and is entitled to a rank among the foremost of its class.—*Minneapolis Tribune.*

The writer tells his story from the Jewish standpoint, and tells it well.—*St. Louis Republic.*

The descriptions of life in Russia are vivid and add greatly to the charm of the book.—*Buffalo Courier.*

A very thrilling story.—*Charleston (S. C.) News.*

Very like the horrid tales that come from unhappy Russia.—*New Orleans Picayune.*

The situations are dramatic; the dialogue is spirited.—*Jewish Messenger.*

A history of passing events in an interesting form.—*Jewish Tidings.*

RABBI AND PRIEST will appeal to the sympathy of every reader in its touching simplicity and truthfulness.—*Jewish Spectator.*

Bound in Cloth.   **Price, Post-paid, $1.**

CHILDREN OF THE GHETTO

BEING

PICTURES OF A PECULIAR PEOPLE.

BY I. ZANGWILL.

OPINIONS OF THE PRESS.

The art of a Hogarth or a Cruikshank could not have made types of character stand out with greater force or in bolder relief than has the pen of this author.—*Philadelphia Record.*

It is one of the best pictures of Jewish life and thought that we have seen since the publication of "Daniel Deronda."—London *Pall Mall Gazette.*

This book is not a mere mechanical photographic reproduction of the people it describes, but a glowing, vivid portrayal of them, with all the pulsating sympathy of one who understands them, their thoughts and feelings, with all the picturesque fidelity of the artist who appreciates the spiritual significance of that which he seeks to delineate.—*Hebrew Journal.*

Its sketches of character have the highest value. . . . Not often do we note a book so fresh, true and in every way helpful.—*Philadelphia Evening Telegraph.*

A strong and remarkable book. It is not easy to find a parallel to it. We do not know of any other novel which deals so fully and so authoritatively with Judæa in modern London.—*Speaker, London.*

Among the notable productions of the time. . . . All that is here portrayed is unquestionable truth.—*Jewish Exponent.*

Many of the pictures will be recognized at once by those who have visited London or are at all familiar with the life of that city.—*Detroit Free Press.*

It is a succession of sharply-penned realistic portrayals.—*Baltimore American.*

TWO VOLUMES.

Bound in Cloth.   Price, postpaid, $2.50.

SOME JEWISH WOMEN.

— BY —

HENRY ZIRNDORF.

OPINIONS OF THE PRESS:

Moral purity, nobility of soul, self-sacrifice, deep affection and devotion, sorrow and happiness all enter into these biographies, and the interest felt in their perusal is added to by the warmth and sympathy which the author displays and by his cultured and vigorous style of writing.—*Philadelphia Record.*

His methods are at once a simplification and expansion of Josephus and the Talmud, stories simply told, faithful presentation of the virtues, and not infrequently the vices, of characters sometimes legendary, generally real.—*New York World.*

The lives here given are interesting in all cases, and are thrilling in some cases.—*Public Opinion* (Washington, D. C.).

The volume is one of universal historic interest, and is a portrayal of the early trials of Jewish women.—*Boston Herald.*

Though the chapters are brief, they are clearly the result of deep and thorough research that gives the modest volume an historical and critical value.—*Philadelphia Times.*

It is an altogether creditable undertaking that the present author has brought to so gratifying a close—the silhouette drawing of Biblical female character against the background of those ancient historic times.—*Minneapolis Tribune.*

Henry Zirndorf ranks high as a student, thinker and writer, and this little book will go far to encourage the study of Hebrew literature.—*Denver Republican.*

The book is gracefully written, and has many strong touches of characterizations.—*Toledo Blade.*

The sketches are based upon available history and are written in clear narrative style.—*Galveston News.*

Henry Zirndorf has done a piece of work of much literary excellence in "SOME JEWISH WOMEN."—*St. Louis Post-Dispatch.*

It is an attractive book in appearance and full of curious biographical research.—*Baltimore Sun.*

The writer shows careful research and conscientiousness in making his narratives historically correct and in giving to each heroine her just due.—*American Israelite* (Cincinnati).

Bound in Cloth, Ornamental, Gilt Top. Price, postpaid, $1.25.

HISTORY OF THE JEWS.

BY

PROFESSOR H. GRAETZ.

Vol.   I. From the Earliest Period to the Death of Simon the Maccabee (135 B. C. E.).
Vol. II. From the Reign of Hyrcanus to the Completion of the Babylonian Talmud (500 C. E.).
Vol. III. From the Completion of the Babylonian Talmud to the Banishment of the Jews from England (1290 C. E.).
Vol. IV. From the Rise of the Kabbala (1270 C. E.) to the Permanent Settlement of the Marranos in Holland (1618 C. E.).
Vol.   V. From the Chmielnicki Persecution in Poland (1648 C. E.) to the Present Time. (In press.)

OPINIONS OF THE PRESS.

Professor Graetz's History is universally accepted as a conscientious and reliable contribution to religious literature.—*Philadelphia Telegraph.*

Aside from his value as a historian, he makes his pages charming by all the little side-lights and illustrations which only come at the beck of genius.—*Chicago Inter-Ocean.*

The writer, who is considered by far the greatest of Jewish historians, is the pioneer in his field of work—history without theology or polemics. . . . His monumental work promises to be the standard by which all other Jewish histories are to be measured by Jews for many years to come.—*Baltimore American.*

Whenever the subject constrains the author to discuss the Christian religion, he is animated by a spirit not unworthy of the philosophic and high-minded hero of Lessing's "Nathan the Wise."—*New York Sun.*

It is an exhaustive and scholarly work, for which the student of history has reason to be devoutly thankful. . . . It will be welcomed also for the writer's excellent style and for the almost gossipy way in which he turns aside from the serious narrative to illumine his pages with illustrative descriptions of life and scenery.—*Detroit Free Press.*

One of the striking features of the compilation is its succinctness and rapidity of narrative, while at the same time necessary detail is not sacrificed.—*Minneapolis Tribune.*

Whatever controversies the work may awaken, of its *noble scholarship* there can be no question.—*Richmond Dispatch.*

If one desires to study the history of the Jewish people under the direction of a scholar and pleasant writer who is in sympathy with his subject because he is himself a Jew, he should resort to the volumes of Graetz.—*Review of Reviews* (New York).

Bound in Cloth.   Price, postpaid, $3 per volume.

SABBATH HOURS.

THOUGHTS.

By LIEBMAN ADLER.

OPINIONS OF THE PRESS.

Rabbi Adler was a man of strong and fertile mind, and his sermons are eminently readable.—*Sunday School Times.*

As one turns from sermon to sermon, he gathers a wealth of precept, which, if he would practice, he would make both himself and others happier. We might quote from every page some noble utterance or sweet thought well worthy of the cherishing by either Jew or Christian. —*Richmond Dispatch.*

The topics discussed are in the most instances practical in their nature. All are instructive, and passages of rare eloquence are of frequent occurrence.—*San Francisco Call.*

The sermons are simple and careful studies, sometimes of doctrine, but more often of teaching and precept.—*Chicago Times.*

He combined scholarly attainment with practical experience, and these sermons cover a wide range of subject. Some of them are singularly modern in tone.—*Indianapolis News.*

They are modern sermons, dealing with the problems of the day, and convey the interpretation which these problems should receive in the light of the Old Testament history.—*Boston Herald.*

While this book is not without interest in those communities where there is no scarcity of religious teaching and influence, it cannot fail to be particularly so in those communities where there is but little Jewish teaching.—*Baltimore American.*

The sermons are thoughtful and earnest in tone and draw many forcible and pertinent lessons from the Old Testament records.—*Syracuse Herald.*

They are saturated with Bible lore, but every incident taken from the Old Testament is made to illustrate some truth in modern life.—*San Francisco Chronicle.*

They are calm and conservative, . . . applicable in their essential meaning to the modern religious needs of Gentile as well as Jew. In style they are eminently clear and direct.—*Review of Reviews* (New York).

Able, forcible, helpful thoughts upon themes most essential to the prosperity of the family, society and the state.—*Public Opinion* (Washington, D. C.).

Bound in Cloth. Price, postpaid, $1.25.

PAPERS

OF THE

Jewish Women's Congress

HELD AT CHICAGO, SEPTEMBER, 1893.

OPINIONS OF THE PRESS.

This meeting was held during the first week of September, and was marked by the presentation of some particularly interesting addresses and plans. This volume is a complete report of the sessions.—*Chicago Times.*

The collection in book form of the papers read at the Jewish Women's Congress . . . makes an interesting and valuable book of the history and affairs of the Jewish women of America and England.—*St. Louis Post-Dispatch.*

A handsome and valuable souvenir of an event of great significance to the people of the Jewish faith, and of much interest and value to intelligent and well-informed people of all faiths.—*Kansas City Times.*

The Congress was a branch of the parliament of religions and was a great success, arousing the interest of Jews and Christians alike, and bringing together from all parts of the country women interested in their religion, following similar lines of work and sympathetic in ways of thought. . . . The papers in the volume are all of interest.—*Detroit Free Press.*

The Jewish Publication Society of America has done a good work in gathering up and issuing in a well-printed volume the "Papers of the Jewish Women's Congress."—*Cleveland Plain-Dealer.*

Bound in Cloth.   **Price, Postpaid, $1.**

OLD EUROPEAN JEWRIES

By DAVID PHILIPSON, D.D.

OPINIONS OF THE PRESS

A good purpose is served in this unpretending little book, . . . which contains an amount and kind of information that it would be difficult to find elsewhere without great labor. The author's subject is the Ghetto, or Jewish quarter in European cities.—*Literary World* (Boston).

It is interesting . . . to see the foundation of . . . so much fiction that is familiar to us—to go, as the author here has gone in one of his trips abroad, into the remains of the old Jewries.—*Baltimore Sun*.

His book is a careful study limited to the official Ghetto.—*Cincinnati Commercial-Gazette*.

Out-of-the-way information, grateful to the delver in antiquities, forms the staple of a work on the historic Ghettos of Europe.—*Milwaukee Sentinel*.

He tells the story of the Ghettos calmly, sympathetically and conscientiously, and his deductions are in harmony with those of all other intelligent and fair-minded men.—*Richmond Dispatch*.

A striking study of the results of a system that has left its mark upon the Jews of all countries.—*San Francisco Chronicle*.

He has carefully gone over all published accounts and made discriminating use of the publications, both recent and older, on his subject, in German, French and English.—*Reform Advocate* (Chicago).

Bound in Cloth   Price, Postpaid, $1.25

JEWISH LITERATURE

AND

OTHER ESSAYS

By GUSTAV KARPELES

OPINIONS OF THE PRESS

There is a very significant sense in which it is impossible really to understand the Bible unless one knows something of the working of the Jewish mind in letters since it was written. One can heartily commend this little volume to people who want this information.—TALCOTT WILLIAMS, *Book News*.

The essays have the charm of an attractive style, combined with a subject of great and varied interest.—*Independent*.

A very informing review of the entire round of Jewish intellectual activity.—*Sunday School Times*.

Its great merit, from the non-Jewish standpoint, is that it looks at civilization and history and literature from a new point of view; it opens unsuspected vistas, reveals a wealth of fact and of opinion before unknown.—*Public Opinion*.

The author shows in every chapter the devoted love for Judaism which prompted the work, and which gave him enthusiasm and patience for the thorough research and study evinced.—*Denver Republican*.

A splendid and eloquent recital of the glories of Jewish religion, philosophy and song.—*Philadelphia Record*.

The result of great research by a careful, painstaking scholar.—*Albany Journal*.

The reader who is unacquainted with the literary life of the highest circles of Jewish society will have his eyes opened to things of which, perhaps, he has never dreamed.—*New Orleans Picayune*.

For popular, yet scholarly treatment, and the varied character of its themes, Dr. Gustav Karpeles' "Jewish Literature and other Essays" is an almost ideal volume for a Jewish Publication Society to issue.—*Jewish Messenger* (New York).

All of the essays show that thorough erudition, clear discernment and criticism for which their author is noted.—*Jewish Exponent* (Philadelphia).

Bound in Cloth. Price, Postpaid, $1.25

Special Series No. 3

THE TALMUD

REPRINTED FROM THE

"LITERARY REMAINS"

OF EMANUEL DEUTSCH

OPINIONS OF THE PRESS

It may be remembered that Deutsch, who was an assistant librarian in the British Museum, first published this paper on the Talmud in the *Quarterly Review* of 1867, and that at once a reputation was made. It was one of the few instances where a single paper in a review made it necessary to publish many editions of the same review.—*New York Times.*

It is the product of a scholarly mind, and it is the genuine exhibit of a world-interesting literary work. *Philadelphia Press.*

In it he has given us a clear and succinct history of the Talmud, with many critical comments and some apt extracts. Being a man of considerable scholarship and fine taste, he has done this work admirably.—*New York Herald.*

Dr. Deutsch's analysis of it [The Talmud] is a standard work.—*Philadelphia Telegraph.*

It gives a large amount of information regarding a very suggestive and fascinating subject.—*San Francisco Call.*

No better idea of the Talmud, with its wealth of legend and occasional gems of poetic thought, could be given in so brief space.—*Milwaukee Sentinel.*

The method of treatment is classical, and at the same time popular.—*Jewish Comment* (Baltimore).

Boards.   Price, Postpaid, 30 Cents

SPECIAL SERIES

No. 1. The Persecution of the Jews in Russia

With a Map
Showing the Pale of Jewish Settlement

Also, an Appendix, giving an Abridged Summary of Laws, Special and Restrictive, relating to the Jews in Russia, brought down to the year 1890.

Paper, - - - - - Price, postpaid, 25c.

No. 2. Voegele's Marriage and Other Tales

BY LOUIS SCHNABEL

Paper, - - - - - Price, postpaid, 25c.

No. 3. THE TALMUD

REPRINTED FROM THE

"LITERARY REMAINS"

OF EMANUEL DEUTSCH

Boards, - - - - - Price, postpaid, 30c.

www.ingramcontent.com/pod-product-compliance
Lightning Source LLC
Chambersburg PA
CBHW022053230426
43672CB00008B/1163